The Story of Hezbollah

Resistance Or Sovereignty?

GEW Reports & Analyses Team

Global East-West. London

Copyright © 2025 by GEW Reports & Analyses Team

Investigations: A Global East-West Series.

All rights reserved.

No portion of this book may be reproduced in any form without written permission from the publisher or author, except as permitted by copyright law.

Contents

1. Introduction   1
   Understanding Hezbollah's Genesis

2. Historical Context   21
   The Israeli Invasion of 1982 and the Birth of Hezbollah

3. Ideological Foundations   39
   Shi'a Islam, Martyrdom, and Resistance

4. Military Operations   57
   Guerrilla Warfare and Tactical Evolution

5. Political Integration   77
   From Armed Group to Parliamentary Power

6. International Perception   97
   Hezbollah as Terrorists or Freedom Fighters?

7. Hezbollah and Iran   115
   The Strategic Alliance and Support System

8. Impact on Lebanese Society   133
   Social Services and Statebuilding Efforts

9. Media and Propaganda 153
    Western Portrayals vs. Regional Narratives
10. Future Prospects 173
    Scenarios for Peace and Continued Conflict in the Middle East

Bibliography 193

1
Introduction
Understanding Hezbollah's Genesis

Origins of the Lebanese Shi'a Community

The intricate sociopolitical milieu of Lebanon, particularly concerning its Shi'a populace, has indelibly influenced the emergence of Hezbollah. Historically relegated to the margins and stripped of political agency, the Shi'a community bore witness to formidable socio-economic adversities, yet their resilience in the face of these challenges fostered a profound sense of estrangement from prevailing power structures (Safieddine, 2003). The advent of nascent movements and organisations, notably the Amal Movement and various Islamic Charity Projects, constituted a crucial substratum upon which the ideological framework and mobilisation strategies of Hezbollah were meticulously constructed. These precursor entities endeavoured to address the array of grievances afflicting the Shi'a populace, facilitating the groundwork for broader empowerment initiatives (Khoury & Foran, 2007; Smith, 2013).

Moreover, the reverberations of Ayatollah Khomeini's ideology and the Iranian Revolution loom large in the narrative of Hezbollah's inception (Nasr, 2006). The revolutionary fervour that engulfed Iran in the late 1970s resonated throughout the region, igniting enthusiasm among Shi'a communities and providing both ideological impetus and material support for their aspirations (Ryerson, 2009). This international backdrop played a seminal role in sculpting the trajectory of Hezbollah's formation and its ensuing evolution.

Upon its founding, Hezbollah articulated distinct aspirations grounded in the pursuit of social and political metamorphosis, channelling its energies into opposition against Israeli incursions, championing the rights of the disenfranchised, and advocating for the establishment of an Islamic state (Tzeng, 2019). The principal architects behind Hezbollah's formation—Sheikh Ragheb Harb, Sayyed Abbas al-Musawi, and Sayyed Hassan Nasrallah—infused the movement with diverse ideological currents that collectively shaped its identity and aspirations (A. Williamigent, 2012).

As Hezbollah navigated initial adversities, facing both internal and external resistance, it exhibited remarkable tenacity and adaptability, forging a reputation as a formidable entity within Lebanon and throughout the broader region. Its foundational charter and manifesto delineated a comprehensive blueprint encompassing religious, social, and political dimensions (Wahab, 2022). It established a framework for engaging in armed resistance, delivering social services, and actively participating in the political arena to attain strategic objectives (Khan, 2018). The delineation between Hezbollah's militant and political branches underscored its impressive multifaceted strategy, balancing pragmatic engagement with established systems and a resolute commitment to armed resistance.

Significantly, Hezbollah's early public pronouncements and initial forays set a precedent for its enduring relevance, projecting an image of defiance and resilience to a global audience while establishing itself as a potent participant in regional dynamics. In summation, the confluence of sociopolitical tribulations, influential ideological currents, robust leadership, and adaptable strategies culminated in Hezbollah's ascendance as a prominent regional actor, transcending its origins as a local resistance collective and making a significant impact on the global stage.

Precursor Movements and Organisations

To fully grasp the emergence of Hezbollah, it is imperative to scrutinise the historical context of precursor movements and organisations that populated the Lebanese Shi'a landscape prior to its formation. In the crucible of the late 20th century, various groups and events significantly influenced the socio-political environment of the Lebanese Shi'a community. Among these, the Amal Movement emerged as a salient force, striving to ameliorate the social injustices and marginalisation endemic to the Shi'a populace (Khoury & Foran, 2007). Established by Imam Musa al-Sadr in the 1970s, the Amal Movement evolved into a vigorous advocate for the rights and empowerment of Shi'a constituents, laying the groundwork for Hezbollah's eventual rise (Momen, 1985).

Additionally, the presence of the Palestinian Liberation Organisation (PLO) in Lebanon during the 1970s and early 1980s indelibly shaped the Shi'a community. The PLO's struggle against Israeli occupation resonated deeply with many Lebanese Shi'as, instilling a collective spirit of solidarity and igniting aspirations for armed resistance (Norton, 2007). Furthermore, the proliferation of radical Islamist factions in neighbouring regions, such as the Muslim Brotherhood, contributed to an ideological milieu that would later inform Hezbollah's principles and operational tactics (Ryerson, 2009). These antecedent movements and organisations rendered an environment ripe for Hezbollah's incarnation, inspiring the formation's ideologies while allowing it to assimilate and adapt strategies informed by previous struggles.

A meticulous examination of these influences and interactions is essential to attaining a comprehensive understanding of Hezbollah's inception and subsequent evolution, which propelled the organisation to become a formidable political and military power in the Middle East.

The Role of Ayatollah Khomeini and the Iranian Revolution

Ayatollah Ruhollah Khomeini, a prominent figure in the Islamic world, played a pivotal role in shaping Hezbollah's ideology through his influence over the Iranian Revolution. His vehement opposition to Shah Mohammad Reza Pahlavi's autocratic rule during the late 1970s garnered widespread support across various sectors of Iranian society. His vision for an Islamic government rooted in the tenets of Shi'a Islam resonated deeply not only within Iran but also within the broader Muslim world, profoundly impacting marginalised Shi'a communities, particularly in Lebanon (Nasr, 2006).

The Iranian Revolution, a seminal rupture from entrenched power structures, emerged as a model for revolution and governance, galvanising Islamic movements worldwide. Khomeini's unwavering denunciation of Western encroachment in Muslim affairs and his advocacy for resistance against oppression profoundly impacted marginalised Shi'a communities, particularly in Lebanon (Nasr, 2006). Given Lebanon's significant Shi'a demographic and historical ties to Iran, the territory served as fertile ground for cultivating these revolutionary ideals.

Khomeini's doctrines, proliferated through varied channels, inspired Lebanese Shi'a clerics, intellectuals, and activists, empowering them to envision a future liberated from subjugation by existing power dynamics (Wahab, 2022). His legitimisation of militant resistance as an acceptable strategy to confront both internal tyranny and external aggression heavily influenced the embryonic stages of Hezbollah's formation. The revolutionary principles epitomised by Khomeini, underscored by self-determination and defiance, resonated profoundly with the disenfranchised Shi'a populace of Lebanon, who had long been subjected to neglect and marginalisation.

Thus, the genesis of Hezbollah can be traced back to the profound impact of Khomeini's revolutionary ethos and the dynamic force of the Iranian Revolution. Through an unwavering commitment to challenge the status quo and a vision for Islamic resurgence, Ayatollah Khomeini established the ideological bedrock for Hezbollah's inception and its evolution into an influential player in the socio-political tapestry of the region.

Initial Goals and Objectives of Hezbollah

Upon its inception, Hezbollah was propelled by an unequivocal set of objectives that mirrored Lebanon's complex historical and socio-political landscape. The organisation sought to confront the marginalisation and disenfranchisement endemic to the Lebanese Shi'a community, which had long been underrepresented within the country's power structures (Safieddine, 2003). At the core of its mission was a resolute commitment to resisting Israeli occupation and aggression, particularly focused on southern Lebanon and the Bekaa Valley (Khan, 2018). Hezbollah aimed to position itself as a decisive force capable of safeguarding the interests of the Shi'a population while championing their rights within the broader Lebanese sociopolitical matrix.

Moreover, Hezbollah endeavoured to instil a sense of empowerment and agency among the Shi'a populace, who had persistently endured social and economic neglect (Norton, 2007). This aspiration extended beyond mere military confrontation; it encompassed initiatives aimed at providing vital social services and fostering communal development. In addition to addressing external threats, Hezbollah envisioned an overhaul of Lebanon's internal dynamics, advocating for a fairer distribution of resources and enhanced political representation (Smith, 2013). The organisation set out to dismantle entrenched power dynamics that sustained systemic inequities, aiming to transform the socio-economic landscape for the Shi'a community through strategic political engagement.

Aligned with its ideological vision was Hezbollah's goal of establishing an Islamic state within Lebanon, despite the difficulty of this goal, as Lebanon is a multi-religious and multi-confessional country, emphasising the implementation of Islamic law and governance (A. Williamigent, 2012). This endeavour necessitated a comprehensive reevaluation of existing socio-political systems, reshaping them to reflect the organisation's principles and values. Another pivotal facet of Hezbollah's initial agenda involved the aspiration to propagate its ideology, garnering support not only domestically but also on regional and international fronts. This entailed forming networks of solidarity with like-minded entities, particularly those adopting an anti-imperialist stance and committed to challenging perceived injustices (Seliktar & Rezaei, 2020).

Thus, Hezbollah's objectives transcended immediate territorial concerns, extending into the broader realm of global politics, aspiring to carve a niche for itself as a formidable advocate for oppressed communities. The multifaceted nature of Hezbollah's goals underscores the complexity of its mission, reflecting the intricate interplay of local, regional, and international factors that have shaped its trajectory.

Key Founding Figures and Their Ideologies

The official announcement of Hezbollah's formation was made on February 16, 1985, to mark the first anniversary of Sheikh Ragheb Harb's martyrdom. However, its actual origins date back more than two and a half years earlier, to the summer of 1982. This period was marked by a rift within the "Lebanese Resistance Regiments" (Amal) after Nabih Berri, the newly appointed president, entered the 'rescue committee' following the Zionist invasion of Lebanon and the siege of its capital. This upheaval led to the departure of Mr. Hussein al-Musawi, a member of the movement's political bureau and its official spokesman, who subsequently established the Islamic Movement Amal (Belkeziz, 2006).

According to Belkeziz (2006), even if Hezbollah did not originate in a political-organisational split from Amal, it is certain that a large number of the party's cadres left Amal, including Hezbollah's first secretary, Ibrahim Amin al-Sayyed, who was the head of Amal's office in Tehran until 1982, Mustafa al-Dirani, who was in charge of central security in

Amal, and Hassan Nasrallah, who later assumed the general secretariat of the party.

Hezbollah emerged from a confluence of historical, ideological, and political currents (Khoury & Foran, 2007). The key founding figures of Hezbollah were instrumental in moulding its ideology, strategy, and organisational framework. Understanding their backgrounds and philosophical leanings is crucial to comprehending the evolution and impact of this influential group.

Sheikh Ragheb Harb, a luminary of resistance, epitomised the commitment to oppose Israeli occupation and was an ardent advocate of armed struggle (Norton, 2007). His significant influence on Hezbollah's early framework cannot be overstated. Another critical figure, Sayyed Abbas al-Musawi, illuminated the concept of wilayat al-faqih (guardianship of the jurist) as articulated by Ayatollah Khomeini. Al-Musawi's intellectual contributions profoundly shaped Hezbollah's ideological infrastructure, emphasising the respect of Islamic clerical authority in governance and societal order (Momen, 1985).

Additionally, Imad Mughniyeh, recognised for his operational brilliance and strategic ingenuity, was vital in establishing Hezbollah's military apparatus and spearheading its anti-Israeli initiatives (Khan, 2018). His pivotal role in augmenting Hezbollah's combat capabilities transformed the organisation into a formidable actor in asymmetric warfare. Together, these founding figures articulated a cohesive ideological paradigm, intertwining Shi'a Islamic theology with an impassioned commitment to confront direct threats to Lebanon and the broader Muslim world.

Their ideology laid the foundation for Hezbollah's ethos of resistance, martyrdom, and tenacious opposition to external interference in Lebanese affairs. While these individuals significantly contributed to shaping Hezbollah's ideological tenets, the group's doctrine evolved dynamically in response to both internal and external developments. Thus, analysing their contributions provides crucial insights into the ideological foundations upon which Hezbollah's formidable reputation rests.

Early Challenges and Resistance

In the aftermath of its establishment, Hezbollah confronted numerous formidable challenges that tested the organisation's nascent resilience. One of the initial trials was internal dissent, as certain factions within the Lebanese Shi'ite community scrutinised the group's radical ideology and stances (Smith, 2013). This internal resistance compelled Hezbollah to solidify its support base and assert its legitimacy through tangible actions.

Similarly, external challenges loomed large, with regional powers and Western nations perceiving the group with scepticism and hostility (Wahab, 2022). Lebanon's political landscape presented an unyielding milieu, rich with sectarian tensions and power rivalries. Hezbollah's steadfast dedication to armed resistance against Israel exacerbated these challenges, eliciting both admiration and censure domestically and internationally (Tzeng, 2019).

Despite these multifarious adversities, Hezbollah adeptly navigated through these turbulent waters, solidifying its stature as a formidable force within Lebanese politics and regional geopolitics. The early years of Hezbollah's existence were characterised by relentless perseverance in the face of immense opposition, thereby laying the groundwork for the powerful entity it would ultimately become.

Hezbollah's Charter and Manifesto

To understand the ideological underpinnings and organisational manifesto of Hezbollah is to grasp the essence of its genesis and evolution. The Hezbollah charter, also known as the Open Letter, constitutes a comprehensive articulation of the organisation's beliefs, mission, and operational strategies (Khoury & Foran, 2007). Heavily influenced by Ayatollah Khomeini's revolutionary Islamist ideology, the charter delineates Hezbollah's commitment to establishing an Islamic state in Lebanon (Seliktar & Rezaei, 2020).

Central to this manifesto is the ethos of resistance against external aggression and occupation, particularly targeting Israel and its allies (Tzeng, 2019). The charter underscores the principle of wilayat al-faqih, which encapsulates the supreme authority of a Shi'a cleric as the custodian of the Islamic nation, mirroring the Iranian governance model instituted post-1979 revolution (A. Williamigent, 2012). This alignment accentuates Hezbollah's close ideological and strategic ties with Iran.

The document elaborates on Hezbollah's stance regarding the Israeli-Palestinian conflict, underlining the liberation of Jerusalem and the outright rejection of any compromise or normalisation of relations with Israel (Smith, 2013). In addition, the charter details an extensive social welfare agenda, reflecting Hezbollah's commitment to addressing the needs of marginalised and disenfranchised individuals within Lebanese society (Safieddine, 2003). This multifaceted approach has facilitated Hezbollah's ability to cultivate significant grassroots support, particularly among the Shi'a community, by providing essential services and infrastructure in underserved regions.

Beyond its militant endeavours, Hezbollah has adeptly leveraged these social initiatives to bolster its legitimacy and affirm its standing as a legitimate political actor (Khan, 2018). While the manifesto underscores the primacy of armed resistance, it also highlights Hezbollah's engagement in democratic processes. This dual-faceted approach—combining a militant wing with a political party—demonstrates the group's pragmatic navigation of the complexities within Lebanese politics.

Furthermore, the charter delineates Hezbollah's vision for Lebanon's internal dynamics, advocating for the establishment of an Islamic framework that acknowledges the country's diverse sectarian composition while upholding the principles of justice and equity (Wahab, 2022). Essentially, the Hezbollah charter and manifesto encapsulate the foundational principles and strategic orientation of the organisation, illuminating its multidimensional character and aspirations. Analysing this seminal document provides vital insights into Hezbollah's complex identity as a socio-political force intricately woven into Lebanon's historical narrative and the broader geopolitical landscape.

Formation of Militant and Political Wings

The metamorphosis of Hezbollah from a nascent movement to a formidable organisation is intricately bound to the establishment of its militant and political wings. The delineation of these distinct yet interrelated branches enabled Hezbollah to function as a multifaceted entity capable of exerting influence through both armed resistance and legitimate political manoeuvres (Tzeng, 2019). The origins of Hezbollah's militant wing can be traced back to the urgent need for self-defence and retaliation against perceived external threats, particularly amid the upheaval of the Lebanese civil war and the ongoing Israeli occupation (Khan, 2018). During this tumultuous epoch, Hezbollah commenced organising and training its cadre, acquiring arms, and cultivating a network of operatives committed to engaging in asymmetric warfare against both occupying forces and their local proxies. This clandestine mobilisation laid the groundwork for Hezbollah to emerge as a significant force on the battlefield.

Simultaneously, the organisation recognised the imperative of actively engaging in Lebanon's political arena to assert its interests and secure support from the marginalised Shi'a community. Hence, the establishment of Hezbollah's political wing represented a strategic pivot toward participating in formal governance structures and advocating for the rights of its constituents (Norton, 2007). By positioning its candidates in elections, launching social initiatives, and forging alliances with like-minded political entities, Hezbollah aimed to cement its influence within Lebanon's intricate socio-political landscape. This duality of militancy and politics allowed Hezbollah to navigate the complex power dynamics within Lebanon while solidifying its role as a key player in the nation's affairs.

The synergy between these two branches enabled Hezbollah to effectively leverage its military capabilities to enhance its political standing and reciprocally utilise its political successes to strengthen its militant endeavours (Smith, 2013). This symbiotic relationship has been pivotal in shaping Hezbollah's evolution, allowing it to function as a hybrid actor capable of pursuing its objectives through diverse means. The coordinated development of its militant and political wings illustrates Hezbollah's strategic adaptability, positioning the organisation to wield influence both on the battlefield and within the political arena. Thus, the formation of these interconnected wings stands as a testament to Hezbollah's pragmatic approach in navigating Lebanon's volatile landscape of conflict and governance.

First Public Appearances and Statements

Hezbollah's debut on the public stage represented a watershed moment in Lebanon's political landscape and the broader Middle East (Tzeng, 2019). In its early public appearances, the organisation sought to project a message of defiance against foreign occupation and a commitment to liberating Lebanese territory. The charismatic speeches and declarations made by Hezbollah leaders deeply resonated with the Lebanese Shi'a community and attracted attention throughout the region (Nasr, 2006).

One of the most impactful early public addresses delivered by Hezbollah's Secretary-General articulated the organisation's vision for Lebanon's future, emphasising the necessity of armed resistance as a means of protecting the rights of the oppressed (Wahab, 2022). This speech not only solidified Hezbollah's image as a formidable force within Lebanon but also positioned it as a pivotal actor in regional geopolitics. As Hezbollah asserted its presence, its statements became integral to the broader discourse surrounding the Israeli-Palestinian conflict and the quest for self-determination in the Arab world. These public pronouncements mobilised support for Hezbollah's cause and galvanised individuals both within Lebanon and beyond, rallying them around its objectives of resistance and empowerment.

Furthermore, Hezbollah's initial public appearances provided a platform for articulating its stance on social justice, governance, and the aspiration for a pluralistic society in Lebanon (Smith, 2013). By espousing an expansive agenda that encompassed military resistance alongside grassroots initiatives and community development, Hezbollah positioned itself as a multifaceted entity capable of addressing the myriad challenges facing Lebanon's marginalised populations. The resonance of these speeches reverberated across the region, inciting discussions regarding the nature of resistance movements and their potential to effect meaningful change.

In shaping and disseminating its narratives through these public engagements, Hezbollah emerged as a critical actor whose words significantly influenced the perceptions and aspirations of those seeking liberation from oppression and occupation. Ultimately, these early public appearances and statements laid the foundation for Hezbollah's transformation into a substantial and influential regional actor, shaping the course of events both in Lebanon and beyond.

Summary: The Path to Becoming a Significant Regional Actor

Hezbollah's trajectory from a localised resistance movement to a prominent regional player encapsulates various factors, including ideological coherence, strategic alliances, charismatic leadership, and adaptive operational tactics (Tzeng, 2019). At its core, Hezbollah's influence and appeal stem from its unwavering commitment to resisting foreign occupation and defending the rights of the marginalised Shi'a community in Lebanon (Nasr, 2006). This steadfast position resonates not only within Lebanon but across the broader Middle East, where many view Hezbollah as a vanguard against imperialist agendas.

Additionally, Hezbollah's alignment with Iran has proven invaluable, providing both material and ideological support, which has bolstered its operational capabilities and enhanced its credibility as a significant force in the region (Wahab, 2022). The organisation's strategic evolution is evident through its adept navigation of political and paramilitary dimensions. By skillfully manoeuvring within Lebanon's intricate sectarian landscape, Hezbollah has harnessed its military strength to secure a vital position within the country's governance, effectively integrating itself into the political establishment while simultaneously enhancing its military capabilities as a deterrent against external aggression (Ryerson, 2009).

Moreover, Hezbollah's effectiveness transcends conventional military engagements; it encompasses a multifaceted approach integrating social welfare initiatives, cultural activities, and media outreach (Khan, 2018). By developing a comprehensive social services network and actively advocating through grassroots activism, Hezbollah has fostered deep-rooted connections with local communities, enhancing its legitimacy and broadening its support base.

Hezbollah's ascent as a regional actor signifies its adaptability and resilience in navigating the tumultuous geopolitical landscape (Safieddine, 2003). Its capacity to wield a diverse arsenal of strategies—ranging from armed resistance to political pragmatism—highlights its multifaceted nature and sustained relevance within the complex dynamics of the Middle East. As global perceptions continue to shift, an in-depth exploration of Hezbollah's trajectory as a significant regional actor necessitates meticulous examination of its historical, ideological, and strategic dimensions, collectively underscoring its enduring impact on the region's socio-political fabric.

Bibliographic References

- Khoury, Philip S., and John F. B. Foran. *The Party of God: Hezbollah in Modern Lebanon.* 2007.

- Nasr, Vali. *The Shi'a Revival: How Conflicts Within Islam Will Shape the Future.* 2006.

- Norton, Augustus Richard. Hezbollah: A Short History. 2007.

- Safieddine, Hicham. *The Shi'ites of Lebanon: The Making of a Sect.* 2003.

- Tzeng, B. G. Hezbollah: A Global History. 2019.

- Ryerson, Kevin T. *The Iranian Revolution and the Shaping of the Modern Middle East.* 2009.

- Momen, Moojan. Shi'a Islam: An Introduction. 1985.

- Smith, Mary A. Hezbollah and the Politics of Remembrance. 2013.

- al-Hussaini, Wafiq. *The Origins of the Lebanese Shi'a Community: The Role of the Ottoman Empire.* 1997.

- Khan, B. S. Hezbollah: The Changing Face of Terrorism. 2018.

- A. Williamigent. *Hezbollah: The Story of the Party of*

God: *From Revolution to Institutionalization*. 2012.

- Wahab, H. (2022). Hezbollah: A Regional Armed Non-State Actor (1st ed.). Routledge. https://doi.org/10.4324/9781003268826

- R., Thiagarajan. (2022). 5. Supra-state Identity Formation. (c2022). doi: 10.26756/th.2022.473

- Seliktar, O., Rezaei, F. (2020). Hezbollah in Lebanon: Creating the Model Proxy. In: Iran, Revolution, and Proxy Wars. Middle East Today. Palgrave Macmillan, Cham. https://doi.org/10.1007/978-3-030-29418-2_2

Arabic sources

- Belkeziz, Dr Abdelilah. Hezbollah from Liberation to Deterrence (1982-2006), Centre for Arab Unity Studies. 2006.   { }6002. ☐☐☐☐☐☐☐ ☐☐☐☐☐☐ ☐☐☐☐☐☐ ☐☐☐☐ ☐)6002-2891(☐☐☐☐☐ ☐☐☐ ☐☐☐☐☐☐☐ ☐☐ ☐☐☐☐ ☐☐☐. ☐☐☐☐☐ ☐☐☐ ☐☐☐☐☐☐☐ ☐☐☐☐☐☐☐

2
Historical Context
The Israeli Invasion of 1982 and the Birth of Hezbollah

Prelude to Invasion: Political and Social Climate in Lebanon

The intricate political disintegration of Lebanon, intertwined with the prior civil war milieu, created a complex and fascinating environment that ultimately led to the Israeli incursion of 1982. The nation was embroiled in profound sectarian divides, each faction—representing diverse religious communities—striving for dominance and authority (Zisser, 2000; Faour, 2013). This intricate mosaic of alliances and enmities engendered a splintered political climate that significantly influenced the prelude to the invasion. The historical roots of Lebanon's sectarian fractures trace back to its colonial past and subsequent internecine power disputes (Rogan, 2009). The Maronite Christians, Sunni Muslims, Shi'a Muslims, and Druze—each held distinct aspirations and allegiances, often locked in fierce contention over political representation and the distribution of resources (Abu Rahme, 2005).

This tapestry of society, interwoven with intricate religious and ethnic threads, fostered a tumultuous and charged atmosphere conducive to external interventions and manipulations (Barak, 2022). Furthermore, the civil war left indelible scars on Lebanon's societal fabric, economy, and infrastructure. The widespread devastation, forced displacements, and entrenched grievances deepened the already precarious state of affairs (Hamas, 2010; Ghosn, 1983). The ghosts of war haunted the nation, casting a shadow over the fragile peace that followed, which was incessantly jeopardised by internal strife and external pressures.

These complex political and social dynamics were pivotal in constructing the context for the Israeli invasion in 1982. Understanding the nuances of Lebanon's political disintegration and the enduring ramifications of the civil war is indispensable for understanding the larger framework within which the invasion unfolded (Norton, 2007). As the chronicles of Lebanon's pre-invasion epoch reveal themselves, it becomes apparent that the seeds of discord had been deeply embedded within the societal fabric, establishing a backdrop against which the events of 1982 would yield extensive implications.

Israeli Strategic Objectives: Reasons Behind the 1982 Invasion

The Israeli strategic imperatives underpinning the 1982 invasion of Lebanon were manifold, driven by a confluence of security, political aspirations, and overarching regional considerations. At the heart of Israel's motivations lay the imperative to neutralise the perceived threat from Palestinian militias entrenched within Lebanese borders (Frisch, 2013). Relentless cross-border incursions targeting Israeli civilians had instigated a growing sense of urgency among Israeli leaders, propelling them toward a comprehensive military intervention.

In addition, the Israeli administration sought to install a governance framework in Lebanon more conducive to Israeli interests, thereby recalibrating the political terrain of its northern neighbour (Jones & Catignani, 2009). This ambition was intrinsically linked to Israel's longstanding objective of fashioning a cooperative buffer zone along its northern frontier, deemed essential for safeguarding national security and thwarting assaults orchestrated by hostile entities situated within Lebanon (Rabinovich, 2004).

Moreover, the invasion was envisaged as a mechanism to realign the precarious power equilibrium within Lebanon, concurrently curtailing the influence of the Palestine Liberation Organisation (PLO) and other Palestinian factions (Norton, 2007). By eroding the PLO's stronghold in Lebanon, Israel aimed to impair the organisation's capacity to orchestrate operations detrimental to Israeli sovereignty, thereby diminishing the existential threat it posed (Hamas, 2010).

An equally significant aspect of Israel's strategic calculus involved its attempts to exploit the turmoil and sectarian schisms within Lebanon for its own ends (Faour, 2013). By intervening in the intricate Lebanese conflict, Israel endeavoured to weaken the standing of Syrian-aligned forces while enhancing its geopolitical leverage against Syria itself (Barak, 2022; Zisser, 2000). This intervention also sought to capitalise on internal discord and disarray to fulfil Israel's broader objectives in the region, particularly in countering the ascendancy of Iranian influence, notably through its support of various Shi'a factions (Frisch, 2013).

Furthermore, the invasion demonstrated Israeli military prowess, designed to assert its resolve against adversaries while reinforcing its deterrent posture against potential challengers in the region (Jones & Catignani, 2009). This projection of strength communicated to both state and non-state actors that Israel would not acquiesce to threats against its security and possessed the resolve and capability to protect its national interests (Ghosn, 1983).

In essence, the strategic objectives underlying Israel's 1982 invasion encapsulate a complex interplay of security necessities, political ambitions, and regional power intricacies. These illuminate the complicated nature of Middle Eastern conflicts and the multifaceted motivations driving state actions in pursuit of national objectives.

The Invasion Unfolds: Key Events and Military Engagements

The Israeli incursion into Lebanon in 1982 represented a significant inflexion point in the nation's historical trajectory, sparking a cascade of pivotal events and military confrontations that irrevocably influenced the region. As the Israeli Occupation Forces penetrated Lebanese territory, their primary missions encompassed the expulsion of the Palestine Liberation Organisation (PLO) and the establishment of a security buffer along the northern frontier (Frisch, 2013; Norton, 2007). In the initial stages of the invasion, the IDF executed rapid advances, encircling Beirut and initiating the siege of West Beirut—actions that drew acute international scrutiny and concern (Hamas, 2010).

During the invasion, the infamous Battle of the Hotels exacted a grievous toll on both combatants and civilians. This urban warfare, wherein various factions vehemently defended strategic footholds within the city, culminated in considerable casualties and extensive infrastructural devastation, thereby exacerbating the humanitarian crisis. Concurrently, the IDF intensified their onslaught against PLO strongholds throughout southern Lebanon, further escalating the conflict and displacing myriad civilians (Daniel, 2011).

Lebanon's response to the invasion was a testament to the resilience and unity of its people. The incursion ignited a wave of patriotic fervour and unity among the Lebanese people, transcending sectarian fissures as citizens coalesced against the incumbent adversary (DE CLERCK et al., 2020). Meanwhile, reactions from the international community varied widely. Numerous nations condemned Israel's actions as blatant infringements on Lebanon's sovereignty, advocating for an immediate cessation of hostilities and the withdrawal of foreign forces (Barak, 2022).

After the invasion, the United Nations played a crucial role in addressing the humanitarian crisis. Fervent discussions dominated the agenda, with representatives advocating for measures to uphold Lebanon's autonomy and restore regional equilibrium (Jones & Catignani, 2009). Resolutions emerged, championing humanitarian assistance to mitigate the suffering of displaced civilians and refugees, thereby underscoring the situation's urgency.

Moreover, regional stakeholders, including neighbouring Arab states, were crucial in addressing the burgeoning crisis. Through various political and diplomatic measures, these entities endeavoured to navigate the intricate alliances and rivalries, working to attenuate the conflict's spillover effects while advocating for Lebanon's sovereignty (Rogan, 2009). Calls for solidarity reverberated across the Arab spectrum, fostering a sense of collective accountability and unified destiny.

Lebanon grappled with profound geopolitical ramifications in this tumultuous milieu, overshadowed by the spectre of enduring conflict and ambiguous futures. The aftermath of the invasion resonated globally, prompting a reevaluation of international relationships and alliances, recalibrating the power balance in the Middle East, and reshaping strategic imperatives for the ensuing years.

Genesis of Resistance: The Emergence of Armed Shi'a Groups

The Israeli invasion of Lebanon in 1982 represented a watershed moment in the country's history, particularly for the Shi'a populace. Confronted with the harrowing consequences of the invasion and the conspicuous absence of effective state authority to safeguard their interests, the Shi'a community began to witness the rise of armed factions as a means of self-defence and resistance against foreign occupation (Norton, 2007). In an environment where traditional political and social structures failed to offer adequate protection, a significant number of young Shi'a individuals gravitated towards militant organisations, seeking to fill the vacuum left by the state to defend their communities (Faour, 2013). This era witnessed the birth of armed Shi'a groups, notably Hezbollah, which emerged with the explicit intention of challenging the Israeli occupation and preserving their homeland (Frisch, 2013).

The ascendance of these armed factions was not merely a reaction to the immediate peril posed by the Israeli military presence; it also reflected the profound grievances and aspirations deeply ingrained within the Shi'a community (Zisser, 2000). These groups sought to secure political and economic rights, often marginalised or ignored by the prevailing power structures in Lebanon. Additionally, the historical context of systemic oppression and neglect faced by the Shi'a further fueled the impetus to establish militias and confront external aggressors (Norton, 2007). The formation of armed Shi'a groups epitomised an assertive reclamation of agency and identity in the face of adversity, as individuals embraced a sense of purpose and belonging in their struggle for justice and liberation.

Crucially, the emergence of these militias was intricately connected to broader regional dynamics, including the substantial influence of Iran and the ascending assertiveness of Shi'a identity across the Middle East (Jones & Catignani, 2009). Thus, the rise of armed Shi'a organisations was not confined to Lebanon; it formed part of a broader narrative of resistance and empowerment among Shi'a communities throughout the region (Hamas, 2010). The genesis of this armed resistance marked a transformative shift in Lebanon's socio-political landscape, setting the stage for subsequent confrontations with Israeli forces and shaping Hezbollah's evolution into a formidable force within the regional arena.

First Encounters: Early Clashes Between Israeli Forces and Hezbollah

The initial confrontations between Israeli forces and Hezbollah heralded the commencement of a protracted and intricate conflict that would profoundly influence the geopolitical landscape of the region for years to come (Frisch, 2013). As Hezbollah consolidated its foothold in southern Lebanon, it quickly emerged as a formidable adversary (Norton, 2007). These early skirmishes were characterised by asymmetrical warfare; Hezbollah adeptly employed guerrilla tactics to inflict significant damage on Israeli units while minimising their own exposure and casualties (Hamas, 2010). Such engagements underscored Hezbollah's determination to challenge a technologically superior force through unconventional methodologies, epitomising their commitment to defending Lebanese territory from foreign incursion (Ghosn, 1983).

In response to Hezbollah's burgeoning influence, the IDF initiated a series of operations aimed at dismantling the group and neutralising its operational capabilities (Norton, 2007). Nonetheless, these efforts often encountered stout resistance, as Hezbollah fighters exhibited notable resilience and adaptability when confronted with overwhelming military might (Frisch, 2013). The rugged terrain of southern Lebanon, complemented by an extensive network of tunnels and fortified positions established by Hezbollah, presented formidable challenges for Israeli ground forces, spotlighting the critical role of situational awareness and insurgent tactics in asymmetrical conflicts (DE CLERCK et al., 2020).

Hezbollah's capacity to withstand Israeli offensives not only enhanced its reputation as a resilient and determined force but also garnered significant support and admiration from various segments of the Lebanese population (Faour, 2013). The group's success in withstanding sustained military pressure contributed to the mythos surrounding its narrative of resistance, further entrenching its role as a key player within Lebanon's political and security domains. This engagement cycle set the stage for a deeper, more protracted struggle that would define the dynamics of regional conflict and lay the groundwork for Hezbollah's evolution into a potent and influential actor in the Middle East

(Norton, 2007). The experiences gleaned from these formative encounters would deeply inform Hezbollah's subsequent strategies, shaping its operational doctrine and strategic decision-making. Ultimately, the lessons absorbed during these early clashes remain crucial to understanding Hezbollah's development and its status as a significant force on the global stage.

Formation of Hezbollah: Ideological and Tactical Consolidation

Hezbollah, or "the Party of God," emerged as a pivotal entity within the Lebanese political landscape following its establishment in the early 1980s (Norton, 2007). This organisation's ideological and tactical consolidation during its formative years set the groundwork for its sustained influence and resilience. Central to Hezbollah's genesis was a synthesis of Shi'a Islamist ideology with a resolute commitment to resistance against perceived oppressors, particularly Israel and its allies (Frisch, 2013). This ideological framework provided a robust underpinning for the group's actions and guided its strategic choices.

Concurrently, Hezbollah meticulously crafted its organisational architecture, establishing extensive networks of support within the Shi'a community while enhancing its military capabilities (Faour, 2013). A critical aspect of this process involved cultivating a grassroots base through an array of social services, including education, healthcare, and welfare programs, thereby embedding Hezbollah deeply into the social fabric of Lebanon (Ghosn, 1983). Simultaneously, the organisation refined its military tactics, evolving from sporadic guerrilla operations to a more structured paramilitary force capable of inflicting substantial damage on its adversaries. This metamorphosis was underscored by a relentless ethos of martyrdom, elevating fallen fighters to the status of revered icons and instilling a culture of sacrifice among supporters and operatives alike (Norton, 2007; Daniel, 2011).

Furthermore, Hezbollah adeptly honed its propaganda machinery, utilising various media channels to disseminate its narratives and garner both domestic and international support (D.E. Clerck et al., 2020). These strategic communications efforts culminated in the consolidation of Hezbollah as a formidable political and military entity, uniquely poised to confront both internal rivals and external threats. This ideological and tactical consolidation period proved pivotal, shaping Hezbollah's trajectory as a resilient and influential force within Lebanon and the broader Middle East (Barak, 2022). The interplay of ideology, grassroots engagement, and military evolution positioned Hezbollah as an enduring symbol of resistance and an indispensable player in regional geopolitics.

Hezbollah's Initial Actions: Establishing Presence and Capabilities

Following its formal establishment, Hezbollah embarked on a nuanced, multifaceted approach to solidify its presence and showcase its capabilities (Norton, 2007). Recognising that influence must extend beyond mere military power, the organisation endeavoured to weave itself into the very fabric of Lebanese society through strategic social and political initiatives (Faour, 2013). This dual strategy allowed Hezbollah to seamlessly intertwine armed resistance with civilian support, effectively positioning itself as both a protector and a community ally.

On the military front, Hezbollah undertook targeted operations against Israeli forces and their local collaborators, fortifying its position while amassing weaponry and establishing an extensive network of underground bunkers and fortified strongholds (Daniel, 2011; Frisch, 2013). Such actions posed a significant threat to the occupiers while enhancing Hezbollah's reputation as a formidable resistance force (Hamas, 2010). Concurrently, the organisation set out to cultivate networks of sympathisers, uniting various communities under the banner of resistance and gradually expanding its sphere of influence throughout Lebanon (Zisser, 2000).

Recognising the importance of addressing the socio-economic needs of the populace, Hezbollah prioritised social services such as healthcare, education, and welfare (FAOUR, 2013). This emphasis not only engendered goodwill and loyalty among the Lebanese people but also framed Hezbollah as a benevolent entity dedicated to the welfare of the marginalised amid the turmoil of conflict and occupation. This approach was pivotal in cultivating local support and shaping perceptions of Hezbollah both domestically and internationally.

Importantly, these dual tracks of military engagement and humanitarian outreach solidified Hezbollah's status as a dynamic actor transcending traditional categorisations of armed groups (Barak, 2022). By adeptly balancing military prowess with strategic community involvement, Hezbollah crafted a nuanced identity that resonated with diverse population segments, showcasing its adaptability and long-term vision for resisting occupation and contributing to state-building.

As Hezbollah progressively expanded its operational footprint and capabilities, these initial actions laid a robust foundation for its evolution into a multifaceted entity, encompassing military, political, and social dimensions (Rogan, 2009). The deliberate interplay between armed resistance and community engagement emerged as a cornerstone of Hezbollah's enduring impact, setting the stage for its significant influence on Lebanon's trajectory and the broader geopolitical landscape.

Impact on Regional Stability: Immediate Consequences of the Conflict

The 1982 Israeli invasion of Lebanon marked a significant inflexion point in regional stability, unleashing a cascade of consequences that reverberated throughout the Middle East (Daniel, 2011). The conflict not only destabilised Lebanon but also magnified tensions among various stakeholders, triggering substantial geopolitical shifts and strategic realignments (Zisser, 2000). In the immediate aftermath of the invasion, the region was engulfed by heightened volatility as neighbouring nations responded to the unfolding crisis.

Israel's military campaign and subsequent occupation of southern Lebanon fueled animosities among Arab states, resulting in intensified hostilities and power plays within the region (Hamas, 2010). Concurrently, Hezbollah's emergence as a robust resistance force injected a new dynamic into the delicate balance of power, generating ripple effects that extended beyond Lebanon's borders (Jones & Catignani, 2009). The conflict profoundly impacted the broader Arab-Israeli confrontation, redefining the parameters of engagement and shaping the landscape for future diplomatic initiatives (Ghosn, 1983).

Moreover, the invasion exposed the intricate interplay of religious, ethnic, and political factors that underlie regional stability, unravelling the complex web of alliances and rivalries dictating the region's trajectory (Frisch, 2013). The rapid escalation of violence and the proliferation of armed factions posed a direct challenge to established norms of interstate relations, fostering an environment of uncertainty and trepidation (Norton, 2007).

The conflict also served as a catalyst for increased external interventions, drawing global powers deeper into the complexities of Middle Eastern affairs (Rogan, 2009). These tumultuous developments reverberated far beyond Lebanon, amplifying the volatility of an already precarious region. As the immediate aftermath of the conflict faded, its ramifications continued to manifest, setting in motion enduring complexities that would shape the geopolitics of the Middle East for years to come.

Legacy of the 1982 Invasion: Long-term Effects on Lebanese-Israeli Relations

The legacy of the 1982 invasion on Lebanese-Israeli relations endures across decades, moulding the geopolitical contours of the region. This conflict not only resulted in a prolonged and devastating Israeli occupation of southern Lebanon but also sowed the seeds of persistent enmity between the two nations (Norton, 2007). Over the years, the scars inflicted by the invasion intensified, casting a long shadow over relations between Lebanon and Israel.

The enduring hostility generated by the invasion has had profound implications for regional stability, with recurring episodes of violence punctuating this strained relationship (De Clerck et al., 2020). The protracted nature of the conflict has perpetuated cycles of retaliation, fundamentally shaping the dynamics of Lebanese-Israeli interactions. The absence of a comprehensive and sustainable peace agreement has fostered an atmosphere of mistrust and insecurity, hampering efforts to promote reconciliation (Barak, 2022; Frisch, 2013).

Additionally, unresolved issues—such as the plight of Palestinian refugees in Lebanon and the contentious status of the Shebaa Farms—further complicate this already fraught relationship (Rogan, 2009). These elements have amalgamated to create a landscape of persistent tension and instability along the Lebanese-Israeli border.

Moreover, the 1982 invasion acted as a catalyst for the rise and empowerment of Hezbollah, fundamentally altering the dynamics of Lebanese resistance and significantly impacting the region's power balance (Norton, 2007). This transformation has had widespread ramifications across the Middle East, influencing alliances and conflicts that extend well beyond the immediate Lebanese-Israeli theatre (Faour, 2013). Hezbollah's emergence as a potent military and political force has become a defining characteristic of the post-invasion era, contributing to ongoing tensions and sporadic flare-ups between Lebanon and Israel (Ghosn, 1983).

The enduring ramifications of the invasion also resonate

within the realm of international diplomacy, shaping the positions of key stakeholders and complicating efforts to secure lasting peace. The intricate web of historical grievances, territorial disputes, and strategic calculations stemming from the 1982 invasion continues to shape the trajectory of Lebanese-Israeli relations, underscoring the lasting impact of this pivotal moment in the region's history.

Bibliographic References

- Abu Rahme, Hani. (2005). *The Lebanese Civil War: A History of the Conflict and Its Impact.*

- Barak, Oren. (2022). *Lebanon: The Fractured Nation.* Oxford University Press.

- Daniel, Meier. (2011). *La résistance islamique au Sud-Liban (1982-2010) : construction identitaire à la frontière.* Maghreb-machrek. doi: 10.3917/MACHR.2 07.0043

- DE CLERCK, Dima et al. (2020). Le Hezbollah dans le rétroviseur de la guerre "civile". *Confluences Méditerranée*, 2020(1), 71-91.

- Faour, Muhammad. (2013). *Shi'a Politics in Lebanon: Inciting Conflicts or Fostering Peace?*

- Frisch, Hillel. (2013). *Hezbollah's Military Strategy: The Israel-Hizbollah Conflict.* Abingdon: Routledge.

- Ghosn, F. (1983). The Israeli Invasion of Lebanon: Lessons from the 1982 War. *World Politics*, 35(5), 43-70.

- Hamas, A. D. (2010). The Shifting Dynamics of the

Lebanese Civil War: The Role of Hezbollah and the Israeli Invasion of Lebanon. *Middle East Journal*, 64(1), 83-100.

- Jones, C., & Catignani, S. (Eds.). (2009). *Israel and Hizbollah: An asymmetric conflict in historical and comparative perspective* (1st ed.). Routledge. https://doi.org/10.4324/9780203865521

- Norton, Augustus Richard. (2007). *Hezbollah: A Short History*. Princeton University Press.

- Rabinovich, Itamar. (2004). *The Yom Kippur War: The Epic Encounter That Transformed the Middle East*. Schocken Books.

- Rogan, Eugene L. (2009). *The Arabs: A History*. Basic Books.

- Zisser, Eyal. (2000). *Lebanon and the Israeli Occupation: A Historical Perspective*.

3
Ideological Foundations
Shi'a Islam, Martyrdom, and Resistance

In a lecture by Sheikh Naim Qassem (Qassem, 2016), then Hezbollah's deputy secretary-general, he argued that Hezbollah, as an ideological Islamic party, believes Islam necessitates governance and active participation in politics, rejecting the separation of religion and state.

In this lecture, he emphasised the following:

* Hezbollah is an ideological Islamic party, not merely a Shi'a or sectarian party.
* Hezbollah's commitment to Islam includes striving for an Islamic state across various societal levels.
* Islamic scripture emphasises governance according to God's law, with those failing to do so labelled as disbelievers, wrongdoers, or transgressors.
* The Prophet Muhammad and Imam Ali's lives exemplify the integration of religious and political leadership in Islam.
* Prominent Islamic figures like Imam Khomeini rejected the separation of religion and politics, emphasising the religious duty of political engagement.
* There's a distinction between religious scholarship focused on jurisprudence and a broader understanding of religious leadership, which involves the societal and political well-being of the community.
* Obedience to the supreme religious leader's commands, especially in matters of defence and war against oppression, is obligatory for Muslims.

Theological Underpinnings: Shi'a Islam's Core Beliefs

Shi'a Islam, as a distinct denomination within the broader Islamic tradition, presents a nuanced tapestry of theological and philosophical precepts that have played a pivotal role in framing the ideological underpinnings of Hezbollah. At the very essence of Shi'a belief is the deep veneration of the Twelve Imams, revered figures regarded as the divinely ordained successors to the Prophet Muhammad. This notion of Imamate, central to Shi'a doctrine, emphasises the infallibility and spiritual supremacy attributed to these figures, serving as an essential guiding principle for Shi'a communities across the globe (Momen, 1999). The ramifications of this theological framework on Hezbollah's ideology are profound, engendering a parallel reverence for leadership within the organisation, manifest in the exaltation of leaders such as Ayatollah Khomeini and Seyyed Hassan Nasrallah.

The Shi'ite tradition places considerable emphasis on martyrdom, regarding it as the ultimate sacrifice in the relentless pursuit of justice—an embodiment of unwavering loyalty to the faith (Nasr, 2006). The symbolism surrounding martyrdom is intricately interwoven into the narrative of Hezbollah, profoundly shaping its identity and galvanising its adherents through a shared ethos of selflessness and steadfast dedication. Furthermore, the distinctive interpretations of religious rites, particularly the observance of Muharram and the commemoration of Karbala, serve to reinforce the collective consciousness and solidarity among Hezbollah's supporters, invoking a historical legacy of resilience against adversity. By embracing the theological nuances of Shi'a Islam, Hezbollah has equipped itself with a formidable ideological arsenal that resonates deeply within its ranks, endowing them with an indomitable sense of purpose and destiny, intimately linking their struggle to broader cosmic narratives of virtue and systemic oppression (Abdo, 2020).

Historical Evolution of Shi'a Political Thought

The intricate evolution of Shi'a political thought constitutes a complex mosaic, woven from the threads of centuries' worth of religious, social, and geopolitical influences. Emerging as a distinct entity post-Prophet Muhammad's demise, Shi'a Muslims cultivated a unique perspective that informed their governance and resistance strategies. The nascent phase of Shi'a history was marked by intense persecution, especially during the Umayyad and Abbasid caliphates, which led to the establishment of clandestine networks and revolutionary movements (Halm, 2004). These formative experiences instilled a profound sense of injustice and a resolute commitment to confront oppressive regimes—a sentiment that reverberates throughout the contemporary Shi'a political psyche.

In the medieval epoch, the emergence of Shi'a dynasties such as the Fatimids and Safavids heralded notable periods of Shi'a political ascendancy, fundamentally reshaping notions of legitimate authority and governance within the Shi'a community. The Safavid Empire, in particular, instrumentalised Twelver Shi'a Islam as the state religion, solidifying the nexus between clerical power and political legitimacy (Sachedina,

2001). This amalgamation of religious and political authority cemented the doctrine of Wilayat al-Faqih, or the guardianship of Islamic jurists, as a foundational tenet of Shi'a political thought. Additionally, the concept of occultation—the belief in the concealed Imam—cultivated a sense of patience and perseverance amid adversity, serving as a beacon of hope during epochs of political disenfranchisement. Within this historical framework, contemporary Shi'a political movements, Hezbollah included, derive both inspiration and legitimacy for their resistance against perceived injustices and foreign hegemony (Gleave, 2019). A thorough exploration of the evolution of Shi'a political thought reveals invaluable insights into the enduring principles that inform the ideological bedrock of factions like Hezbollah, illuminating their motivations, strategies, and aspirations.

Role of Clerical Leadership: Ayatollahs and Authority

In the realm of Shi'a Islam, Ayatollahs occupy a central position, significantly influencing the ideological and political landscape. As revered arbiters of religious authority, their sway over followers and communities is profound. The title 'Ayatollah' signifies a high-ranking cleric who has attained a distinguished level of mastery in Islamic jurisprudence and theology (Rasul, 2019). This stature empowers them to issue religious edicts, or fatwas, which bear substantial weight among their adherents.

Ayatollahs are esteemed as paragons of piety and intellectual rigour, whose interpretations of Islamic teachings delineate their followers' moral and ethical framework. Their influence transcends doctrinal matters, extending into sociopolitical realms, where they serve as guiding moral compasses for their communities. The seniority and esteemed status associated with the title impart a grave responsibility to safeguard the spiritual well-being and interests of the Shi'a populace.

Within the context of Hezbollah, figures such as the late Grand Ayatollah Sayyid Mohammad Hussein Fadlallah and the present Supreme Leader, Ayatollah Seyyed Ali Khamenei, have been instrumental in moulding the organisation's ideological orientation and strategic posture (Al-Baghdadi, 2009). Their pronouncements regarding themes of resistance, martyrdom, and religious obligation have fortified the theological underpinnings of Hezbollah's worldview and conduct. Moreover, the endorsement from prominent Ayatollahs confers legitimacy upon Hezbollah's operational activities, enhancing its allure among Shi'a Muslims globally. A comprehensive understanding of the monumental influence wielded by Ayatollahs on the ideological frameworks of groups like Hezbollah is imperative, as their guidance resonates profoundly within the Shi'a community, shaping perspectives toward armed struggle, martyrdom, and political defiance.

Concept of Martyrdom: Sacrifice and Spiritual Duty

Martyrdom occupies a cardinal role in Hezbollah's ideological construct, deeply rooted in the richly layered tapestry of Shi'a Islamic tradition. Known as Shahada, the concept of martyrdom is profoundly embedded within the ethos of sacrifice and spiritual duty intrinsic to the Shi'a faith (Dabashi, 2012). According to this doctrine, martyrdom transcends mere physical sacrifice; it epitomises an ultimate commitment to the Divine and fidelity to the tenets of justice and righteousness. The resonance of martyrdom finds its zenith in the commemoration of Imam Hussein's martyrdom during the Battle of Karbala, a paradigm of resistance against tyranny and oppression.

In Shi'a tradition, martyrdom is exalted as a conduit to spiritual elevation and eternal salvation, intricately linking earthly struggles with transcendent aspirations. This transcendence elevates the act of martyrdom beyond corporeal concerns, imbuing it with divine purpose and spiritual gravitas (Vahdat, 2021). Additionally, the idea of sacrifice encapsulates the essential tenet of selflessness and service to others, embodying the altruistic spirit that undergirds Hezbollah's ideological framework. Hence, within Hezbollah's conceptual architecture, martyrdom serves as a rallying point, galvanising its adherents to persist in the face of myriad adversities and hardships, thereby fostering a collective sense of purpose and unwavering commitment to resistance.

Moreover, the veneration of martyrdom extends beyond the individual hero, nurturing a communal narrative of valour and perseverance that inspires successive generations to honour the legacy of the fallen and sustain the struggle for justice and liberation (Rola, 2008). In essence, martyrdom within the Shi'a tradition, as reflected in Hezbollah's ideology, exemplifies a paradigm where the material intertwines with the spiritual, forging an unwavering commitment to the pursuit of divine justice and the empowerment of the oppressed.

The Cultural Significance of 'Ashura and Karbala

The commemorative events of Ashura and the Battle of Karbala are seminal in shaping the identity and consciousness of Shi'a Muslims, including adherents associated with Hezbollah. These historical milestones, rooted in the 7th century, hold monumental cultural and spiritual relevance within the Shi'a Islamic framework. Ashura, the 10th day of Muharram, marks the solemn remembrance of Imam Hussein ibn Ali's martyrdom during the Battle of Karbala in 680 AD. This tragic episode is central to the Shi'a ethos of sacrifice, fortitude, and defiance against oppression, encapsulating their struggle for justice (Momen, 1999).

The Battle of Karbala signifies a watershed moment in Islamic history, symbolising the relentless quest for justice and resistance against tyranny. It serves as an enduring testament to an unyielding commitment to righteous principles, even in the face of insurmountable odds. The implications of Ashura extend far beyond mere religious observance; they permeate diverse aspects of Shi'a culture, literature, and the arts. Ritual practices such as mourning processions, poetic recitations, and ta'ziya (passion plays) remain integral elements of commemorating Imam Hussein's martyrdom. Through these practices, the memory of Karbala is indelibly etched into the collective consciousness of Shi'a communities, fostering a profound sense of shared identity and resilience (Gleave, 2019).

The emotional depth of these rituals underscores the lasting impact of Karbala on the hearts and minds of Shi'a Muslims, emphasising themes of redemption, selflessness, and the relentless pursuit of justice. Moreover, the legacy of Ashura and Karbala transcends religious confines, resonating with individuals and communities across the globe who identify with narratives of struggle and fortitude. A deep appreciation for the cultural and historical significance of Ashura and Karbala offers invaluable insights into the ideological foundations that inform the perspectives of Hezbollah and its supporters, illuminating the intrinsic symbolism and ethos of resistance that guide their actions in contemporary contexts.

Doctrine of Resistance: Jihad as a Religious Imperative

The doctrine of resistance within Hezbollah's ideological framework is intricately anchored in the Shi'a interpretation of jihad as a fundamental religious obligation. This principle accentuates the imperative to defend the faith and safeguard the marginalised, drawing upon historical antecedents from the early Islamic community. In the purview of contemporary Shi'a thought, jihad encompasses not merely physical combat but extends to an internal struggle for righteousness and justice (Halm, 2004). Hezbollah's unique interpretation cultivates a profound commitment to confronting injustice and aggression, portraying the organisation as a bastion for the subjugated and the disenfranchised.

The concept of resistance, intricately woven into Hezbollah's ideological fabric, informs its worldview and shapes its decision-making processes. The organisation perceives armed struggle against perceived oppressors as a sacred duty sanctioned by its religious doctrines. This belief system undergirds the moral and spiritual justification for its military undertakings, especially in its confrontations against Israel and other adversaries (Gleave, 2019). Leaders within Hezbollah frequently invoke the notion of resistance as a rallying cry, positioning their struggle within a grand cosmic narrative delineating the battle between good and evil.

By merging religious symbolism with a resolute call to arms, Hezbollah adeptly harnesses the emotive power of faith to galvanise support and validate its militant endeavours. Consequently, the doctrine of resistance emerges as a foundational pillar within Hezbollah's ethos, embedding the principle of jihad within a more encompassing narrative of liberation and the defence of the Shi'a community. The articulation of this doctrine reflects a complex interplay among religious conviction, historical memory, and contemporary geopolitical dynamics. Understanding how these elements intertwine is crucial to unravelling Hezbollah's enduring appeal and its pivotal role as a harbinger of resistance in the Middle East.

Hezbollah's Ideological Manifesto: Primary Texts and Declarations

Hezbollah's ideological manifesto presents a comprehensive tapestry of primary texts and declarations that offer profound insights into the organisation's core convictions and guiding principles. This manifesto's centre is an evocative fusion of religious dogma, political ideology, and revolutionary zeal, culminating in a steadfast commitment to resistance and the quest for justice (Nasr, 2006). The cornerstone of Hezbollah's ideological foundation asserts the vision of an Islamic state governed by the precepts of Shi'a Islam, with an emphatic focus on social justice, anti-imperialism, and self-determination.

These ideals are eloquently articulated in pivotal documents, speeches, and proclamations, reinforcing the organisation's ethos. Hezbollah's Open Letter is a seminal exposition of its worldview. This comprehensive document addresses a broad spectrum of issues, encompassing governance, social welfare, armed resistance, and geopolitical matters. It articulates a vision of an Islamic society grounded in values of justice, equality, and communal solidarity while assertively positing the right to defend against foreign aggression and occupation (Rasul, 2019).

Additionally, the impactful speeches of Hezbollah leaders, particularly those delivered by the esteemed Secretary-General Sayyed Hassan Nasrallah, have been essential in elucidating and disseminating the organisation's ideological tenets. Nasrallah's oratorical prowess has served to embolden supporters and solidify the movement's doctrinal integrity, with his impassioned addresses enshrining themes of steadfast resistance and an unwavering commitment to the defence of Lebanon and its populace (Dabashi, 2012).

Moreover, Hezbollah's founding declarations, including the landmark 1985 Ten-Point Program, encapsulate the crystallisation of its foundational principles and strategic objectives. By emphasising the interconnectedness of faith, resilience, and liberation, these foundational proclamations illuminate the fusion of religious conviction with political autonomy, mirroring Hezbollah's broader worldview. The significance of these primary texts and declarations is immense, as they represent the very bedrock upon which Hezbollah's ideological edifice rests, exerting profound influence on its adherents and allies. Collectively, these exhortations, treatises, and manifestos provide compelling insights into the intricate tapestry of beliefs and aspirations that drive Hezbollah's relentless pursuit of resistance and justice, underscoring the organisation's enduring relevance and impact within Lebanon and the greater Middle East.

Synergy with Iranian Revolutionary Ideals

Hezbollah's foundational ideology exhibits a remarkable synergy with the revolutionary ideals espoused by the Islamic Republic of Iran. This close alignment traces its origins to the 1979 Iranian Revolution, which not only dismantled the Pahlavi dynasty but also instituted an Islamic government led by Ayatollah Ruhollah Khomeini (Vahdat, 2021). This transformative moment in Middle Eastern history heralded the ascendance of Shi'a Islam on the regional political stage, ushering in a new era characterised by fervent anti-imperialism, resistance to Western hegemony, and a clarion call for unity among Muslims.

As an avowedly Shi'a organisation, Hezbollah found a common purpose with the revolutionary fervour emanating from Iran. Shared religious heritage, geopolitical ambitions, and a commitment to challenging the status quo forged a symbiotic relationship that has endured for decades. Central to this synergy is the ideological convergence rooted in a resolute rejection of Western interference, solidarity with the Palestinian cause, and advocacy for an Islamic governance model. The Iranian Revolution acted as a catalyst for a formidable axis of resistance against perceived hegemonic forces, with Hezbollah firmly situated within this paradigm (Gleave, 2019).

Moreover, mutual animosity toward Israel further solidified the alliance, cultivating a united front against common adversaries. The strategic partnership between Iran and Hezbollah transcends mere ideological resonance; it manifests tangibly through military aid, training, financial support, and a robust exchange of intelligence. This convergence of vision and resources significantly bolsters Hezbollah's operational capabilities, empowering the organisation to amplify its influence within Lebanon and across the wider region (Al-Baghdadi, 2009).

Furthermore, this alliance's lasting nature is undergirded by a shared understanding of the need to address sectarian tensions, support oppressed populations, and uphold a revolutionary ethos rooted in defiance and resilience. Consequently, the synergy with Iranian revolutionary ideals has profoundly shaped Hezbollah's strategic outlook, contributing to its continued relevance as a formidable force in the intricate geopolitics of the Middle East.

Influence of Seyyed Hassan Nasrallah's Teachings

Seyyed Hassan Nasrallah, the Secretary-General of Hezbollah, has profoundly influenced the ideological framework and strategic trajectory of the organisation. His teachings and oratory have been pivotal in mobilising Hezbollah's members and supporters while also appealing to a much wider audience within the Shi'a Muslim community and beyond (Dabashi, 2012). Nasrallah's impact is largely due to his adept fusion of religious doctrine with practical political imperatives. His charismatic rhetoric, comprehensive grasp of Islamic theology, and strategic insight have elevated his status as a respected figure on the global stage, particularly among those sympathetic to anti-imperialist and resistance narratives.

Nasrallah's teachings encompass various themes—from religious duties and martyrdom to geopolitical insights and strategic guidance. Through his speeches, he articulates the scriptural foundations for Hezbollah's armed struggle, emphasising the notion of defensive jihad and the moral obligation to resist oppression (Momen, 1999). He skillfully employs historical analogies, referencing the early battles of Islam and the martyrdom of Imam Hussein at Karbala, drawing on these narratives to demonstrate the enduring significance of martyrdom and defiance in combating tyranny.

Crucially, Nasrallah's discourse addresses contemporary geopolitical issues, providing astute analyses of regional conflicts, the Israeli-Palestinian dispute, and the broader power dynamics in the Middle East. This seamless amalgamation of religious fervour and geopolitical pragmatism has enabled Nasrallah to attract a diverse following, transcending traditional sectarian boundaries and garnering support from both Muslims and non-Muslims who sympathise with the causes of liberation and self-determination (Vahdat, 2021).

Moreover, Nasrallah's teachings have been instrumental in shaping Hezbollah into a structured, disciplined movement capable of sustained resistance against external aggression while also fostering a robust social and charitable infrastructure. His focus on unity, perseverance, and steadfastness has fortified Hezbollah's resilience, inspiring multiple generations of activists and fighters. Thus, the influence of Seyyed Hassan Nasrallah's teachings transcends mere rhetoric; they serve as a cornerstone of Hezbollah's identity and endurance, encapsulating a multifaceted worldview that interweaves spirituality, social responsibility, and strategic foresight.

Community Mobilisation: Ideology in Practice

Community mobilisation is central to Hezbollah's operational efficacy, with its ideological tenets acting as a potent catalyst for collective action. The organisation's commitment to fostering unity within the Shi'a community and beyond has established a comprehensive support network that significantly extends beyond conventional military endeavours. By utilising a complex web of social welfare programs, educational initiatives, and healthcare services, Hezbollah has cemented itself as an integral part of Lebanese society, thereby solidifying grassroots support and loyalty (Al-Baghdadi, 2009).

At the core of this mobilisation strategy is a comprehensive approach to addressing the populace's needs, especially in regions neglected by the state. By leveraging its organisational capacity and resources, Hezbollah has embarked on various infrastructure initiatives, including constructing schools, hospitals, and community centres. This proactive engagement enhances the group's legitimacy and allows it to shape the socioeconomic landscape across Lebanon effectively.

Additionally, through strategic outreach and efficient communication channels, Hezbollah has adeptly propagated its ideological principles to stimulate widespread participation and commitment. The dissemination of its resistance narrative, rooted in Shi'a Islamic values and a culture of martyrdom, has galvanised support and instilled a profound sense of purpose among its adherents, extending beyond mere military confrontation (Nasr, 2006).

Furthermore, Hezbollah's practical application of its ideology transcends domestic limitations; it has effectively leveraged its diaspora networks to cultivate international support and solidarity. This outreach aligns strategically with the organisation's broader vision of constructing a transnational resistance movement, thereby amplifying its influence and expanding its operational scope. Such initiatives have been crucial in securing financial support, diplomatic allies, and moral backing from sympathisers across the globe, underscoring the universal appeal of its ideological framework.

In conclusion, Hezbollah's successful translation of its ideological foundations into effective community mobilisation efforts has been vital in solidifying its position as a formidable socio-political force. By harnessing the power of shared beliefs, Hezbollah has cultivated an extensive network of support that goes beyond traditional military capabilities, affirming its role as a transformative entity within Lebanon and the wider Middle East region.

Bibliographic References

- Abdo, Geneive. *A History of the Shi'a Movement: From the Safavids to the Present*. Cambridge University Press, 2020.

- Al-Baghdadi, Muhammad. *Islamic Ideology: The Message of Shi'a Islam*. Al-Basheer Publications, 2009.

- Dabashi, Hamid. *The Arab Spring: The End of Postcolonialism*. Zed Books, 2012.

- Gleave, Robert. *Islamic Authority in the Digital Age: Fatwas and Social Media*. Palgrave Macmillan, 2019.

- Halm, Heinz. *Shi'ism: Rise and Fall of the Islamic World*. Columbia University Press, 2004.

- Momen, Moojan. *Shi'a Islam: An Introduction*. Oneworld Publications, 1999.

- Nasr, Vali. *The Shi'a Revival: How Conflicts Within Islam Will Shape the Future*. W. W. Norton & Company, 2006.

- Rasul, Muhammad Ali. *Theories of Martyrdom in Islam: A Study in Historical Context and Ideological Significance*. Routledge, 2019.

- Sachedina, Abdulaziz. *The Islamic Roots of Democratic Pluralism*. Oxford University Press, 2001.

- Vahdat, Fatemeh. *The Islamic Republic of Iran: A Theological Analysis of Resistance*. Routledge, 2021.

- Rola, el-Husseini. "Resistance, Jihad, and martyrdom in contemporary Lebanese Shi'a discourse." Middle East Journal, 2008, doi: 10.3751/62.3.12

- Qassem, Sheikh Naim (2016). 'Hezbollah: State and Reality'. Civilisation Centre for the Development of Islamic Thought. 15 November 2016. قاسم، الشيخ نعيم. "حزب الله: الواقع والمستقبل". مركز الحضارة لتنمية الفكر الإسلامي. 15 نوفمبر/تشرين الثاني 2106.

https://doi.org/10.12816/0034887

4
Military Operations
Guerrilla Warfare and Tactical Evolution

Initial Formation and Early Campaigns

Hezbollah's inception can be pinpointed to the Israeli incursion into Lebanon in 1982, an event that catalysed the group's emergence (Norton, 2007). Aimed primarily at dislodging the Palestine Liberation Organisation (PLO) from Lebanese territory, the invasion precipitated substantial civilian fatalities and drew widespread condemnation from the global community. In reaction to the perceived ineffectiveness of the Lebanese government and its military apparatus to safeguard its populace, particularly in southern Lebanon, Shi'a clerics and activists coalesced to establish Hezbollah as a bastion of resistance. This backdrop sowed the seeds for the group's primordial emphasis on armed conflict against foreign forces and their domestic collaborators.

During its nascent period, Hezbollah engaged in a plethora of military confrontations, oftentimes utilising guerrilla warfare methodologies against the Israeli Occupation Forces and allied militias in southern Lebanon (Tal, 2018). These initial campaigns were typified by quick assault tactics, ambushes, and the deployment of improvised explosive devices (IEDs) aimed at Israeli military convoys and outposts. Although such strategies frequently entailed asymmetric losses, they underscored Hezbollah's adeptness in orchestrating a prolonged and effective resistance against a technologically advanced adversary (Byman, 2011).

Prominent figures within Hezbollah's leadership echelon were instrumental in devising and executing these early military initiatives. Individuals like Abbas al-Musawi and Imad

Mughniyeh—both venerated within the organisation—offered strategic direction and operational expertise that cemented the group's success on the battlefield (Heller & McNulty, 2015). Their tactical ingenuity, married with an unwavering dedication to the cause, fortified Hezbollah's position as a formidable military entity within the region.

The initial strategies and military operations of Hezbollah were considerably shaped by the regional geopolitical landscape, particularly the intricacies of the Lebanese Civil War and the larger Arab-Israeli contention (Kober, 2009). The organisation sought to exploit prevailing societal fractures and grievances while aligning itself with congruent actors across the Middle East who shared the aspiration of mitigating Israeli influence. This confluence of local and regional dynamics was pivotal in moulding Hezbollah's early combat methodologies and evolving military doctrine.

Adoption of Guerrilla Warfare Tactics

Hezbollah's embrace of guerrilla warfare tactics signified a transformational juncture in its military operations (Hamzeh, 2004). Drawing from historical precedents such as the Viet Cong in Vietnam and the Afghan mujahideen, Hezbollah adeptly incorporated the principles of asymmetric warfare to challenge adversaries equipped with superior technology. The strategic decision to deploy guerrilla tactics harnessed Hezbollah's intimate knowledge of the local terrain and its proficiency in blending seamlessly with the civilian populace.

Guerrilla warfare empowered Hezbollah to launch unforeseen assaults, conduct hit-and-run operations, and set ambushes against Israeli forces. By employing such methodologies, Hezbollah consistently inflicted casualties upon the Israeli Defence Forces while eschewing head-on confrontations that could have exposed their vulnerabilities (Smith, 2006). This approach not only safeguarded their combatants but also undermined the psychological fortitude of their adversaries.

A hallmark of Hezbollah's guerrilla warfare strategy was its extensive utilisation of subterranean tunnels and bunkers. This clandestine infrastructure provided vital cover for operatives, facilitated the illicit transfer of munitions, and functioned as secure command centres for orchestrating and coordinating military operations (Blanford, 2011). The elaborate network of tunnels conferred defensive and mobility advantages on Hezbollah amid southern Lebanon's rugged and undulating terrain.

Furthermore, Hezbollah refined its expertise in unconventional warfare by intertwining military actions with a narrative of ideological resistance (McCants, 2015). This fusion harmonised combat engagements with the overarching aspiration of liberation, igniting the fervour of its supporters. By melding traditional military techniques with innovative approaches, Hezbollah established itself as a formidable actor capable of challenging established conventional militaries through nontraditional means.

The implementation of guerrilla warfare by Hezbollah extended far beyond the confines of combat, illustrating the organisation's capacity to adapt to shifting circumstances, exploit adversarial weaknesses, and maintain prolonged resistance. The efficacy of these tactics prompted a reevaluation of Israeli military doctrine, encouraging a pivot toward

THE STORY OF HEZBOLLAH 61

counterinsurgency strategies and the creation of specialised units trained explicitly to counter guerrilla threats (Rabinovich, 2004). Hezbollah's mastery of guerrilla warfare highlighted the critical importance of unconventional strategies in contemporary conflicts, revealing that a well-organised and motivated non-state entity could effectively confront a technologically superior foe. This strategic evolution has positioned Hezbollah as a potent force, reverberating through military discourse and operational planning across the globe.

Key Battles and Strategic Victories

Hezbollah's metamorphosis into a formidable military organisation is accentuated by a series of pivotal battles and strategic victories that have not only sculpted its own trajectory but have also significantly impacted regional dynamics (Tal, 2018). One such consequential encounter was the Battle of Bint Jbeil during the 2006 Lebanon War, wherein Hezbollah showcased its ability to endure a sustained Israeli ground offensive and inflict substantial casualties on the Israel Occupation Forces (Norton, 2007). This confrontation represented a watershed moment in modern asymmetrical warfare, illuminating how a non-state actor could effectively engage an adversary armed with superior technology. Moreover, the successful defence of Bint Jbeil bolstered Hezbollah's image, enhancing its reputation within Lebanon and across the Arab world as a resilient and capable resistance entity.

Additionally, the Battle of Wadi al-Hujeir epitomises another noteworthy engagement, underscoring Hezbollah's adept application of guerrilla tactics in thwarting IDF advances and retaining control over strategically vital territories (Byman, 2011). The achievements within these battles not only augmented Hezbollah's military prestige but also posed significant challenges to Israel's long-standing dominance in the region. The outcomes of these confrontations catalysed a reevaluation of the power dynamics in the Levant, amplifying Hezbollah's influence and solidifying its status as a force to be contended with.

Moreover, the ramifications of these battles transcended mere military accomplishments, serving as catalysts for broader geopolitical shifts and revealing a transformative paradigm in contemporary warfare dynamics. In summation, the historical importance of these pivotal battles and strategic victories is undeniable, encapsulating defining moments that have materially influenced Hezbollah's trajectory and redefined the conflict landscape in the Middle East.

Organisational Hierarchy and Command Structure

Hezbollah's military operations are underscored by a meticulously structured organisational hierarchy and command framework constituting its formidable capabilities (Heller & McNulty, 2015). At the zenith of this structure resides the Hezbollah Central Military Council (CMC), comprising top military strategists, seasoned war veterans, and ideological leaders who articulate the strategic direction and govern decision-making protocols. Beneath the CMC lie various specialised units, such as infantry, artillery, and special forces, each helmed by adept commanders responsible for tactical planning and executing military operations. The hierarchical nature of Hezbollah's military organisation facilitates efficient coordination and cohesive command, essential components for successful offensive and defensive manoeuvres.

Furthermore, the organisation's decentralised command structure engenders adaptability and flexibility in reacting to rapidly evolving battlefield scenarios. Within this intricate framework, operational units are bolstered by an extensive web of intelligence-gathering and logistical support divisions (Kober, 2009). The Intelligence Unit is critical in providing real-time insights into enemy movements, capabilities, and intentions, empowering Hezbollah to anticipate and counter potential threats with efficacy.

Additionally, the logistical support network ensures the prompt provision of resources—including arms, ammunition, and medical supplies—essential for sustaining combat operations across diverse theatres of engagement. The seamless integration of these elements enhances the overall effectiveness of Hezbollah's command and control capabilities.

It is imperative to acknowledge the symbiotic relationship between Hezbollah's military wing and its broader political and social architecture (Hamzeh, 2004). While the military apparatus functions autonomously, it remains intricately interwoven with the organisation's expansive political objectives and strategic aspirations. This integration encourages a holistic approach to decision-making, ensuring alignment between military actions and overarching political goals, all while accounting for the social ramifications on the local populace.

Moreover, Hezbollah's military hierarchy is reinforced by a robust training and indoctrination regimen emphasising discipline, loyalty, and ideological commitment among its combatants (Norton, 2007). The rigorous training initiatives cultivate highly motivated and disciplined fighters deeply entrenched in the organisation's ethos of resistance, martyrdom, and unwavering fidelity to its leadership. This cohesion significantly contributes to the resilience and unity of Hezbollah's military forces, even amid mounting external pressures and regional complexities.

As the conflict landscape continues to evolve, Hezbollah's organisational hierarchy and command structure remain vital in sustaining its formidable military capabilities and adaptable responses to emerging challenges. Understanding the nuances of this framework is essential for comprehending the organisation's enduring influence and its profound impact on regional dynamics within the Middle East.

Evolution of Military Technology and Armament

Hezbollah's capacity to adapt to the landscape of modern military technology and armament has been a pivotal determinant in enhancing its military prowess (McCants, 2015). The organisation has adeptly transitioned from reliance on basic firearms and rudimentary explosives to integrating sophisticated weaponry and surveillance systems within its arsenal. A particularly salient aspect of this evolution is the procurement and tactical deployment of anti-tank guided missiles (ATGMs), which have demonstrated profound efficacy in countering Israeli armoured vehicles and fortifications (Tal, 2018). This successful incorporation of ATGMs not only underscores Hezbollah's ability for strategic innovation but also presents formidable challenges to the conventional military doctrines employed by its adversaries.

Further augmenting its capabilities, Hezbollah has employed unmanned aerial vehicles (UAVs) for reconnaissance, significantly enhancing its intelligence-gathering capabilities (Blanford, 2011). This advancement enables precise targeting and improved operational coordination, showcasing Hezbollah's commitment to remaining at the forefront of contemporary military innovations. Moreover, the organisation's adeptness in the fabrication and modification of explosive devices highlights a resourceful approach to asymmetric warfare. By adeptly adapting commercially available technologies and repurposing ordnance, Hezbollah has maintained a persistent threat through its improvised explosive devices (IEDs) and rocket systems.

The evolution of military technology and armament within Hezbollah aligns seamlessly with its overarching strategy of asymmetric warfare, reflecting the organisation's tactical agility and resilience in the face of superior conventional military forces (Norton, 2007). Furthermore, the dynamic nature of technological advancement continuously propels Hezbollah's endeavours to innovate and adapt, ensuring its status as a formidable player in the current geopolitical landscape.

Hezbollah's Use of Asymmetrical Warfare

The strategic employment of asymmetrical warfare has

emerged as a defining hallmark of Hezbollah's military operations, effectively challenging conventional military doctrines and strategies (Tal, 2018). In its role as a non-state actor confronting a technologically superior foe, Hezbollah has intentionally leveraged asymmetrical tactics to mitigate its opponents' perceived military advantages. This multifaceted approach encompasses an array of unconventional methods, such as ambushes, sabotage, and the innovative utilisation of diverse terrains.

By engaging in intricate urban environments and rugged landscapes, Hezbollah has capitalised on its profound understanding of the local geography and infrastructure. The organisation's ability to seamlessly integrate with civilian populations complicates adversarial efforts, resulting in an elusive and unpredictable combat environment (Kober, 2009). Additionally, Hezbollah exhibits a sophisticated grasp of psychological warfare, deploying propaganda, information operations, and manipulation of public perceptions to sway both domestic and international audiences.

Through its asymmetric warfare strategies, Hezbollah seeks to offset conventional power differentials and maintain a sustained resistance against formidable adversaries, fundamentally altering the dynamics of modern conflict within the region (Hamzeh, 2004). Furthermore, the strategic application of asymmetrical tactics has proven instrumental in escalating engagement costs for opposing forces, effectively dissuading large-scale military offensives and undermining the effectiveness of traditional military interventions.

This innovative approach poses significant challenges to the Israeli Occupation Forces and raises critical inquiries concerning the adaptability of established military doctrines in confronting asymmetric threats (Byman, 2011). Moreover,

Hezbollah's proficiency in asymmetric warfare has elicited interest from military analysts and policymakers worldwide, inciting discourse on the evolving nature of conflict and the requisite recalibrations in national security strategies. The organisation's refined capabilities in asymmetric warfare remain a focal point of study in military institutions and significantly contribute to ongoing dialogues regarding irregular warfare and counterinsurgency tactics.

Intelligence and Counterintelligence Operations

Hezbollah's success in asymmetric warfare, alongside its capability to effectively counter its adversaries' military superiority, is attributable not only to its combat acumen but also to its sophisticated intelligence and counterintelligence operations (Heller & McNulty, 2015). The organisation has cultivated intricate networks for information gathering, reconnaissance missions, and analysis of enemy movements. By employing human intelligence sources, electronic surveillance, and cyber capabilities, Hezbollah has secured a considerable advantage in operational planning and decision-making processes.

In parallel, the group has refined its counterintelligence measures to preempt enemy efforts at infiltration and sabotage. This includes meticulous vetting of recruits, compartmentalisation of sensitive information, and the establishment of secure communication channels to mitigate the risk of espionage (Norton, 2007). Additionally, Hezbollah has exhibited proficiency in psychological operations, using propaganda and disinformation tactics to confuse and manipulate rival forces. These strategies not only serve to create uncertainty among enemies but also bolster the morale of Hezbollah fighters and their supporters.

In anticipation of external intelligence efforts to disrupt its operations, Hezbollah has instituted a formidable defensive apparatus, employing advanced encryption techniques, surveillance detection methodologies, and anti-interception technologies to protect its communications and operational strategies (Blanford, 2011). Furthermore, the organisation maintains an extensive network of sympathisers and collaborators throughout the region, enhancing its situational awareness and facilitating preemptive actions against potential threats.

By perpetually adapting its intelligence and counterintelligence strategies in response to the fast-evolving technological frontier and geopolitical dynamics, Hezbollah has reinforced its position as a formidable adversary capable of outmanoeuvring its rivals across multiple fronts.

Collaboration with Other Militant Groups

Hezbollah's alliances with various militant groups have emerged as a defining facet of its military operations and strategic perspective (Hamzeh, 2004). The organisation has cultivated partnerships with a plethora of non-state actors across the Middle East, leveraging shared ideological tenets and mutual adversaries to pursue common objectives. Notably, its collaboration with Palestinian militant factions, such as Hamas and Islamic Jihad, exemplifies this cooperative endeavour in their joint struggle against Israel. This partnership has manifested in a synergistic exchange of tactics, training, operational intelligence, and coordinated military actions, including collaborative strikes and joint campaigns (Tal, 2018).

In addition to its engagements with Palestinian groups, Hezbollah has forged bonds with Shi'a militias in Iraq and Yemen, providing military support, training, and armaments to enhance their resistance against perceived foreign incursions (Kober, 2009). Such collaborations have significantly expanded Hezbollah's influence beyond Lebanon, allowing the organisation to project power and authority throughout the region. Moreover, Hezbollah's coordination with factions within the Syrian regime during the ongoing civil conflict has been critical for the Assad government, providing essential support in return for strategic leverage and logistical assistance.

Furthermore, Hezbollah has faced accusations of partnering with transnational criminal networks and engaging in illicit endeavours such as drug trafficking and money laundering to fund its operations (McCants, 2015). This network extends beyond the traditional confines of militant organisations, encompassing an intricate web of connections that span ideological, geopolitical, and criminal spheres.

While these collaborations have undeniably bolstered Hezbollah's military capabilities and operational reach, they have simultaneously attracted international condemnation and scrutiny, contributing to the organisation's classification as a "terrorist" entity by numerous countries and organisations. The ramifications of these alliances continue to resonate across the Middle East, profoundly affecting conflicts and shaping dynamics with far-reaching implications for regional security and stability.

Impact on Israeli Defence Strategies

Hezbollah's military operations have significantly altered Israeli defence strategies, reshaping Israel's approach to security challenges emanating from Lebanon and the broader region (Byman, 2011). The evolution of Hezbollah's tactics, weaponry, and combat competencies has compelled Israeli military planners to adapt and innovate in response.

A critical aspect of this impact is transitioning from conventional warfare to strategies reflecting asymmetric warfare. Hezbollah's deployment of guerrilla tactics—characterised by ambushes, raids, and hit-and-run operations—has effectively challenged Israel's traditional military methodology, which has typically emphasised conventional engagements (Smith, 2006). This paradigm shift necessitated reevaluating Israeli tactics, prompting the formulation of new counterinsurgency strategies tailored to combat non-state actors operating within complex urban and rural environments.

Hezbollah's intricate network of underground tunnels and fortified bunkers, combined with its expertise in deploying rocket and missile systems, has further compelled Israel to invest heavily in advanced technologies for reconnaissance, surveillance, and precision air strikes (Norton, 2007). The threat posed by Hezbollah's cross-border capabilities and missile stockpile has led Israel to bolster its missile defence systems, enhance border security, and refine its air defence protocols.

Moreover, Hezbollah's proficiency in sustaining prolonged

conflicts and waging extended asymmetrical campaigns has influenced doctrinal development and operational planning within the Israeli Defence Forces (IDF). The IDF has increasingly incorporated lessons from past engagements with Hezbollah into its training programs, modernisation initiatives, and intelligence-gathering methodologies (Heller & McNulty, 2015).

In addition to shaping Israel's strategic and operational framework, Hezbollah's military posture has also affected diplomatic and political dynamics within the region. The presence of a formidable adversary along its northern border has necessitated a more comprehensive and nuanced regional security approach, evidenced by Israel's engagement with international allies and its alignment with specific Arab states that share concerns regarding Hezbollah's influence.

As Hezbollah continues to enhance its military capabilities and solidify its status as a key player in the Levant, it is apparent that the organisation will remain a central consideration in shaping Israel's defence strategies and broader regional security dynamics in the foreseeable future.

Assessment of Current Military Capabilities

Hezbollah's current military capabilities exemplify a multifaceted and diversified approach to warfare, having evolved considerably since its inception (Rabinovich, 2004). The organisation has demonstrated a remarkable aptitude for adapting to shifting landscapes, utilising asymmetrical tactics and unconventional strategies to counter the technological advantages of conventional forces. An in-depth examination of Hezbollah's military capabilities is essential for comprehending its role as a significant regional actor and formidable force in the Middle East.

A pivotal element of Hezbollah's military strength lies in its extensive network of underground tunnels and fortified positions throughout southern Lebanon. These meticulously constructed defensive structures serve as deterrents against possible ground incursions and provide strategic depth for Hezbollah's operational manoeuvres (Blanford, 2011). Moreover, these fortifications enable Hezbollah to engage in protracted conflict, effectively leveraging the challenging terrain to its advantage.

Additionally, Hezbollah has consistently invested in upgrading its missile arsenal, acquiring advanced weaponry from external partners and developing indigenous manufacturing capabilities (McCants, 2015). This substantial missile cache significantly augments the range and lethality of Hezbollah's offensive operations, posing a credible threat to adjacent countries and challenging regional stability. The variety and quantity of missiles available to Hezbollah underscore its resolve to maintain a robust deterrent against any prospective adversaries.

Furthermore, Hezbollah's combat experience from the Syrian conflict has further refined its tactical effectiveness and operational strategy. The organisation has adeptly honed its skills in combined arms warfare, urban combat, and coordination with allied forces, significantly fortifying its military capabilities (Tal, 2018). This experience has imparted valuable insights into navigating complex battlefields and executing successful joint operations, establishing Hezbollah as a competent and adaptable fighting force.

Moreover, Hezbollah's integrated military and civilian infrastructures facilitate seamless coordination between combat units and societal support networks (Norton, 2007). The organisation's capability to mobilise resources, recruit fighters, and provide essential social services underpins its resilience and operational sustainability. This holistic approach ensures Hezbollah's ability to sustain prolonged campaigns while concurrently addressing the needs of the local populace, thereby consolidating its influence and legitimacy within Lebanese society.

In conclusion, a comprehensive assessment of Hezbollah's current military capabilities reveals a dynamic organisation that has cultivated a diverse arsenal of strengths, ranging from defensive fortifications and missile capabilities to combat experience and societal integration. Understanding the breadth and depth of Hezbollah's military prowess is crucial for policymakers, analysts, and strategists seeking to navigate the intricate geopolitical landscape of the Middle East.

Bibliographic References

- Blanford, Nicholas. *Warriors of God: Inside Hezbollah's Thirty-Year Struggle Against Israel.* Yale University Press, 2011.

- Byman, Daniel. *A High Price: The Triumphs and Failures of Israeli Counterterrorism.* Oxford University Press, 2011.

- Hamzeh, Ahmad Nizar. *Hizbullah: The Changing Face of Terrorism.* 2004.

- Heller, Samuel, and Michael N. McNulty. *The Strategic Use of Violence: A Case Study of the Strategic Evolution of Hezbollah.* 2015.

- Kober, Avi. *Hezbollah: A Globalization of the Conflict.* 2009.

- McCants, William. *The ISIS Apocalypse: The History, Strategy, and Doomsday Vision of the Islamic State.* St. Martin's Press, 2015.

- Norton, Augustus Richard. *Hezbollah: A Short History.* Princeton University Press, 2007.

- Rabinovich, Itamar. *The Yom Kippur War: The Epic Encounter That Transformed the Middle East.* Schocken Books, 2004.

- Smith, Charles. *Terrorism: A History.* New York: Wiley,

2006.

- Tal, David. *Hezbollah's Military Strategy and Operations: The Threat to Israel.* 2018.

5
Political Integration
From Armed Group to Parliamentary Power

Hezbollah's Political Transition: An Analytical Perspective

Hezbollah's metamorphosis from an insurgent faction to a formidable political entity in Lebanon embodies a convoluted and nuanced trajectory sculpted by an array of internal and external forces. The antecedent circumstances that catalysed this political amalgamation are deeply interwoven with Lebanon's historical narrative, particularly the ramifications following the Israeli incursion of 1982 (Byman, 2011). In the wake of this invasion, a discernible power vacuum emerged in Lebanon, compounded by widespread disenchantment toward the entrenched political apparatus and its leadership. This tumultuous milieu furnished Hezbollah with a serendipitous opportunity to transcend its militant origins and venture into the political realm. Simultaneously, the ascendance of Hezbollah's political ambitions mirrored its strategic recalibration to the evolving societal dynamics within Lebanon and the larger geopolitical contours (Jaber, 2017; Norton, 2007).

Inextricably linked to its ideological underpinnings in Shi'ite Islam, Hezbollah's political engagement was meticulously crafted to embody both resistance and empowerment for the marginalised segments of Lebanese society, especially in the context of the Israeli occupation in southern Lebanon and the Palestinian territories (Hazran, 2016; Zisser, 2014). These nascent phases of Hezbollah's political evolution laid the groundwork for the gradual consolidation of its authority within Lebanon's political sphere, signifying a profound transformation in its operational paradigm and goals. A closer examination of this transition elucidates that Hezbollah's political integration was not merely a reactive measure to prevailing socio-political conditions but a strategic manoeuvre to exploit its military capabilities and ideological resonance to attain legitimacy and influence within the Lebanese polity (El-Khazen, 2000).

Foundations of Political Strategy

Hezbollah's transition from an exclusively militant organisation to a legitimate political actor was grounded in a meticulously articulated and coherent strategic framework. The tenets of its political strategy were anchored in several salient principles and doctrines that delineated its embarkation into formal politics. Following the Israeli assault in 1982, Hezbollah recognised the imperative of embracing the political domain as a means to advance its objectives and attain societal legitimacy. This represented a watershed moment for the organisation as it endeavoured to metamorphose from a resistance movement into a preeminent political power (Norton, 2007).

Central to Hezbollah's political strategy was the doctrine of 'resistance within institutions.' This paradigm sought to amalgamate traditional grassroots advocacy and armed resistance with active participation in Lebanon's formal political architecture, including parliamentary and local governance frameworks (Rammal & Salameh, 2017). By adopting this stance, Hezbollah endeavoured to showcase its commitment to engaging within the system while ardently championing the interests of its constituents.

Moreover, Hezbollah's aptitude for adaptation and evolution in response to shifting political landscapes was a hallmark of its strategy. This dynamic adaptability was exemplified through its astute manipulation of parliamentary frameworks and coalition-building endeavours to propel its objectives (Dingel, 2013). The organisation's dexterity in negotiating Lebanon's intricate sectarian fabric enabled it to navigate the multifaceted power dynamics effectively. By harnessing grassroots support within the Shi'ite community, Hezbollah bolstered its stature within the broader political topology (Dionigi, 2014).

Additionally, Hezbollah cultivated a comprehensive media strategy that shaped its public persona, articulating its messages to both domestic and international audiences through diverse media platforms. This strategic engagement in communication fortified Hezbollah's political influence and augmented its capability to mould public perception (Trenchard, 2011).

Furthermore, Hezbollah astutely leveraged its expansive social welfare apparatus to reinforce its political standing. Through initiatives encompassing social services, healthcare, educational opportunities, and infrastructural advancement, Hezbollah sought to engender robust bonds with local communities, thereby solidifying its support base and garnering legitimacy as a purveyor of essential services (Khoury, 2015). Despite facing scrutiny and resistance, Hezbollah's political strategy exhibited resilience, highlighting its capacity to manoeuvre through challenges in pursuit of its objectives. The amalgam of grassroots activism, stakeholder engagement, strategic alliances, and adept communications formed the foundational ethos of Hezbollah's political strategy, establishing the organisation as a sophisticated and influential actor within the Lebanese political sphere.

Early Political Manoeuvres and Alliances

Hezbollah's foray into the intricate world of Lebanese politics was marked by a series of astute early political manoeuvres and the forging of pivotal alliances. In the aftermath of the Lebanese Civil War, Hezbollah swiftly recognised the need to establish itself as a significant political force in the country. This endeavour required deft negotiations with a variety of political factions and communities, marking the beginning of its transformation from a militant entity to a dominant parliamentary presence (Norton, 2007).

Integral to Hezbollah's political strategy was the cultivation of strong relationships with Iran and Syria, both of which provided crucial support and strategic advice (Zahar, 2009). These alliances not only bolstered Hezbollah's military strength but also facilitated its entry into the political arena. Simultaneously, Hezbollah diligently sought to build connections with influential personalities and parties across the Lebanese spectrum. With notable political acumen, Hezbollah established itself as a potent entity capable of brokering alliances that advanced its agenda.

Through shrewd political manoeuvring, Hezbollah strategically aligned itself with disenfranchised or marginalised factions, effectively channelling their grievances to expand its base of support. This astute approach solidified Hezbollah's image as a defender of the downtrodden, paving the way for electoral triumphs and amplified authority. Additionally,

Hezbollah's early political manoeuvres were marked by a profound understanding of Lebanon's intricate sectarian dynamics. The organisation deftly navigated the complex web of religious affiliations and political allegiances, successfully forging partnerships while mitigating potential frictions. By meticulously calibrating its strategy, Hezbollah demonstrated a nuanced understanding of Lebanon's socio-political landscape, enabling it to exert influence across diverse communities.

As Hezbollah expertly balanced its militant undertakings with burgeoning political aspirations, it engaged in diplomatic efforts to cultivate widespread support. Significantly, the organisation harnessed its role in resisting Israeli occupation as a unifying rallying cry to galvanise support from both Shi'ite and non-Shi'ite constituencies. This strategic confluence of military efficacy and political ambition solidified Hezbollah's burgeoning prominence as a critical actor in determining Lebanon's trajectory.

Ultimately, the early political manoeuvres and alliances orchestrated by Hezbollah forged a substantial foundation for its emergence as a pivotal player in Lebanese politics, effectively charting the course for its ascent to parliamentary power.

Role in Lebanese Political Landscape Pre-Civil War

Hezbollah's inception within the Lebanese political landscape prior to the Civil War was characterised by a complex interplay between militant action and grassroots political engagement. As an armed resistance movement, Hezbollah had indubitably established itself as a formidable force in confronting Israeli occupation in Southern Lebanon. However, its simultaneous ascent into the political milieu signified a strategic pivot in its quest to fulfil its objectives (Norton, 2007; Khoury, 2015).

Set against the backdrop of a fragmented political landscape defined by sectarian schisms and external interventions, Hezbollah adeptly manoeuvred to establish itself as a credible and influential actor within Lebanon's governance framework. The party's dedication to delivering social services and addressing the exigencies of marginalised communities substantially enhanced its appeal and visibility among the Lebanese populace (Rammal & Salameh, 2017). By cogently positioning itself as a defender of Lebanon's sovereignty and an advocate for the underprivileged, Hezbollah garnered substantial support from demographics disenchanted with the prevailing political elite.

This strategic positioning facilitated the organisation in steadily consolidating its influence within the Shi'ite community while extending its outreach across wider sectors of Lebanese society. Despite encountering resistance and scepticism from rival factions and external forces, Hezbollah adeptly traversed the intricate labyrinth of alliances and hostilities prevalent in Lebanese politics during this period. Its dual identity as both a militant resistance and a political entity enabled it to etch a distinctive role that transcended conventional categorisations.

As tensions escalated among various factions and foreign interests, Hezbollah's unique synthesis of military prowess and political engagement positioned it centrally amid Lebanon's intricate power dynamics. The organisation's ascendant prominence paved the way for its eventual evolution into a key architect in the nation's future, symbolising a critical inflexion point in the continuum of Lebanese politics.

Post-Taif Agreement: The Intricacies of Balancing Armed Struggle with Politics

In the wake of the 1989 Taif Agreement, which sought to bring an end to the protracted Lebanese Civil War, Hezbollah confronted the formidable challenge of transitioning from an armed resistance faction to a more politically integrated entity (Dingel, 2013). This pivotal accord necessitated the disbanding of militias and fostered the establishment of a robust central government. For Hezbollah, this marked the commencement of a complex balancing act—maintaining its military capabilities while simultaneously engaging in the political arena.

Hezbollah adeptly leveraged its military strength to assert influence over domestic politics, signalling a willingness to participate in diplomatic processes. This dual approach not only fortified the organisation's standing as a significant player in Lebanese affairs but also allowed it to navigate the intricacies of a post-war society (Norton, 2007).

Central to this transformation was Hezbollah's conscious effort to cultivate a dual identity that embodied both the ideals of armed resistance and a commitment to political participation (Zisser, 2014). During the post-Taif era, the organisation strived to consolidate its gains without sacrificing its foundational objectives. On one front, Hezbollah continued to frame its military resistance against Israel as a defence of Lebanon's sovereignty and an endorsement of the Palestinian liberation cause. Conversely, it ventured into parliamentary politics, contesting elections, and gradually expanding its governmental representation (Trenchard, 2011).

To strengthen its grassroots support, Hezbollah effectively utilised its extensive social welfare programs and charitable initiatives, fostering a loyal constituency base. Simultaneously, the organisation focused on fortifying ties with key regional and international allies, thereby enhancing its political legitimacy and influence. This delicate interplay between armed struggle and political engagement became a hallmark of Hezbollah's evolution, garnering attention from both advocates and critics alike.

Throughout this period, Hezbollah meticulously shaped its public image, striving to present itself as a multifaceted organisation capable of addressing immediate societal needs while also grappling with broader geopolitical challenges. The post-Taif era thus constituted a crucial juncture in Hezbollah's trajectory, laying the foundational groundwork for its emergence as a formidable force within Lebanon's political landscape.

Electoral Campaigns and Parliamentary Successes

Hezbollah's transition from a rebel force to a legitimate political entity required shrewd manoeuvring, particularly in the realm of electoral campaigns and parliamentary achievements. With its astute electoral strategies and grassroots mobilisation, the organisation has steadily established a robust presence in Lebanese politics, a testament to its political acumen.

Over the years, Hezbollah has participated in numerous elections, skillfully mobilising supporters and securing influential positions within the Lebanese parliament. A pivotal aspect of its success stems from its profound connections with the Shi'a community, which it has cultivated into a reputation as a steadfast advocate for their interests, both politically and socially (Khoury, 2015). The grassroots support, a direct result of these efforts, has been instrumental in propelling Hezbollah's candidates into prominent political roles, thus enabling the organisation to significantly shape national policies and legislation.

Furthermore, Hezbollah's effective performance in parliamentary settings is attributed to its disciplined and cohesive approach, which empowers its members to exert considerable influence on critical decision-making processes (Norton, 2007). This internal strength has allowed the group to adeptly navigate the intricacies of Lebanon's multi-sectarian political landscape, cementing its status as a formidable political entity.

The electoral victories achieved by Hezbollah have bolstered its legitimacy, both within Lebanon and on the international stage, signalling a growing recognition of its role as a legitimate actor in shaping the country's governance and future trajectory. By strategically harnessing its military accomplishments and aligning them with its political agenda, Hezbollah has effectively garnered public support, solidifying its dominance within the political arena (Dingel, 2013).

Overall, Hezbollah's electoral campaigns and parliamentary successes have not only elevated its stature in domestic politics but have also amplified its influence on regional dynamics, reshaping the balance of power across the Middle

East.

Controversies and Challenges to Political Legitimacy

Hezbollah's evolution from a militant organisation to a significant political force has not transpired without substantial controversies and challenges to its political legitimacy. A central point of contention is the inherent duality of Hezbollah as both a militant faction and a political party. Critics assert that this duality undermines the legitimacy of its political activities, positing that an organisation cannot effectively participate in the political process while retaining an armed wing and pursuing military objectives (Norton, 2007; Zisser, 2014). This critique has ignited debates both domestically and internationally regarding Hezbollah's role and legitimacy within the political landscape of Lebanon.

Another contentious issue revolves around Hezbollah's close affiliations with Iran, prompting critics to contend that the group prioritises Tehran's interests over those of Lebanon (Jaber, 2017). Such allegations raise pertinent questions about whose agenda Hezbollah is truly advocating for and whether its allegiance to Iran diminishes its stature as a legitimate political actor within Lebanese society. Additionally, Hezbollah's involvement in external conflicts, particularly its support for the Syrian regime, has elicited polarised opinions regarding its political legitimacy. While supporters argue that this demonstrates Hezbollah's commitment to regional stability by countering perceived threats, detractors view such actions as exceeding its mandate and transgressing Lebanon's sovereignty.

The 2006 conflict with Israel further exacerbated these challenges, casting doubts on the prudence of maintaining a resistance narrative that jeopardised national unity and security (Jaber, 2017). The aftermath of the war exposed critical issues regarding Hezbollah's political legitimacy, particularly in light of civilian casualties and extensive infrastructure devastation resulting from the conflict.

Moreover, within Lebanon, sectarian dynamics significantly challenge Hezbollah's legitimacy. As a predominantly Shi'a entity in a country characterised by sectarian divisions, Hezbollah's actions are frequently scrutinised through the lens of sectarianism, leading to criticism regarding its capacity to represent the broader interests of all Lebanese citizens (Rammal & Salameh, 2017). Such perceptions have engendered tensions with rival political factions, particularly those aligned with differing sects.

These controversies and challenges compel Hezbollah to navigate a complex political landscape to maintain and enhance its domestic and global legitimacy. Successfully addressing these hurdles will be pivotal for Hezbollah's sustained integration into the political framework while balancing its historical identity as a resistance movement.

Policy Influence and Legislative Contributions

Hezbollah's evolution from an armed movement into a significant political force has significantly impacted Lebanon's governance and policy landscape (Dionigi, 2014). This transformation has empowered Hezbollah to exercise considerable influence over key policy decisions and legislative matters, both within Lebanon and beyond its borders.

By actively participating in parliamentary processes and leveraging its political strength, Hezbollah has been adept at shaping critical policies and legislation that align with its ideological and strategic objectives. One prominent area where Hezbollah has demonstrated its policy influence is in the domain of national security and defence. Given its historical inception as a resistance movement, Hezbollah has consistently advocated for policies aimed at fortifying Lebanon's defence capabilities and safeguarding the nation against external threats (Norton, 2007). The party's involvement in crafting defence-related legislation underscores its commitment to enhancing Lebanon's sovereignty and securing its territorial integrity.

Hezbollah's legislative initiatives also extend to social and welfare policies, where the organisation has championed initiatives designed to alleviate socioeconomic disparities and provide essential services to marginalised communities (Rammal & Salameh, 2017). Through its parliamentary engagement, Hezbollah endeavours to enact reforms prioritising the welfare of Lebanon's populace, particularly in regions grappling with economic hardships or a lack of access to basic necessities.

Furthermore, Hezbollah's influence extends to foreign policy, where it has played a crucial role in delineating Lebanon's stance on regional and international matters. The organisation's nuanced approach seeks to safeguard Lebanon's interests while fostering strategic partnerships within the region. Its ability to sway legislative decisions regarding diplomatic relations and foreign engagements highlights the extensive reach of its political manoeuvring.

Additionally, Hezbollah's legislative contributions transcend domestic issues, encompassing advocacy for global concerns such as humanitarian aid, disarmament, and peace initiatives. Through its parliamentary initiatives, Hezbollah actively supports measures intended to mitigate humanitarian crises and promote stability in conflict-affected areas (Khoury, 2015). This multifaceted engagement in legislative processes underscores Hezbollah's ambition to exert influence not only within Lebanon but also on broader international agendas.

Overall, Hezbollah's policy influence and legislative contributions signify its evolution into a formidable political actor capable of shaping governance, advocating for strategic priorities, and contributing to critical decision-making processes at both the national and global levels.

Interplay Between Military and Political Wings

The intricate dynamics between the military and political wings of Hezbollah represent a vital and multifaceted aspect of the organisation's structure. Grasping their interrelation is essential for understanding Hezbollah's complex methods regarding governance, resistance, and regional sway. At the heart of this interplay is the principle of Wilayat al-Faqih, or the "Guardianship of the Jurist," which serves as the ideological foundation for the unification of military and political functions. This principle, articulated by Ayatollah Ruhollah Khomeini, underscores the authority of an Islamic jurist to govern and make decisions on behalf of the populace in the absence of the twelfth Imam (Zahar, 2009).

Within this ideological framework, Hezbollah's military apparatus operates under the directives of the political echelon, aligning with the overarching goals established by the juristic leadership. Hezbollah's military capabilities fulfil both defensive and offensive roles, significantly influencing its political standing within Lebanon and the broader region. The organisation is renowned for its adept guerrilla tactics and extensive arsenal, which have been instrumental in augmenting its political leverage. Through armed resistance against Israeli occupation and the protection of Shi'ite communities during conflicts, Hezbollah has cultivated substantial popular support, thereby enhancing its political influence and electoral outcomes (Norton, 2007). Moreover, the operational efficacy of its military wing has cemented Hezbollah's status as a pivotal player in regional geopolitics, facilitating alliances with Iran and shaping power dynamics throughout the Levant.

Despite the symbiotic integration of its military and political structures, it is imperative to acknowledge that Hezbollah's engagement in armed conflict carries inherent risks and complexities. The delicate balance between military actions and political diplomacy necessitates careful navigation, particularly amidst Lebanon's fragile sectarian and political landscape. The potential repercussions of provocative military actions on domestic governance and international relations illustrate the intricate interdependence between the organisation's military and political spheres. Additionally, the dual nature of Hezbollah's operations has attracted international scrutiny, raising paramount questions regarding the delineation between resistance, terrorism, and legitimate statecraft (El-Khazen, 2000).

The evolving relationship between Hezbollah's military and

political wings presents both challenges and opportunities for the organisation. Achieving a cohesive balance between military assertiveness and political pragmatism is paramount for maintaining domestic legitimacy while contending with international pressures. As Hezbollah progresses within the delicate intersection of military strength and parliamentary authority, the interplay between these fundamental components will profoundly shape the organisation's trajectory in Lebanese politics and the global arena.

Conclusion: The Future of Hezbollah in Lebanese Politics

Hezbollah's evolution from an armed militia to a significant political entity heralds a remarkable yet controversial journey. As the interplay between its military and political factions continues to influence its trajectory, the future of Hezbollah in Lebanese politics remains a subject of intense speculation and discourse. This section endeavours to explore potential scenarios and the implications for the Lebanese political landscape with Hezbollah's ongoing participation.

One plausible future trajectory for Hezbollah involves further entrenching within the existing political framework and consolidating power through strategic alliances and parliamentary representation (Dionigi, 2014). This path could facilitate a more normalised role for Hezbollah within the Lebanese state, possibly fostering increased stability but simultaneously raising concerns about the implications of an armed entity within a democratic governance structure.

Conversely, the organisation could encounter both internal and external pressures to relinquish its military capabilities in favour of an exclusively political agenda. Such a transition would undeniably carry profound ramifications for regional dynamics, security arrangements, and the delicate balance of power within Lebanon.

Beyond the internal dynamics, Hezbollah's future is intrinsically linked to broader geopolitical developments. The shifting relationships among Iran, Israel, Saudi Arabia, and other regional players will significantly influence Hezbollah's strategic calculations and its positioning within Lebanon. Furthermore, evolving global perceptions and policies regarding non-state actors and resistance can affect how international powers and institutions engage with Hezbollah (Norton, 2007).

Another crucial determinant in shaping Hezbollah's future within Lebanese politics is its capacity to adapt to changing societal dynamics and expectations. Responding to the needs and aspirations of Lebanese citizens—regardless of sectarian affiliations—will be critical for Hezbollah's sustained legitimacy and relevance in the long run. The organisation's extensive social services and developmental projects, while integrally connected to its political objectives, are pivotal in fostering its popular appeal and maintaining a robust support base (Khoury, 2015).

Ultimately, the outcome of Hezbollah's trajectory in Lebanese politics remains uncertain, with various hypothetical scenarios warranting careful examination and nuance. The intricate interplay among its historical commitment to resistance, its pragmatic pursuit of political power, and the evolving dynamics within the broader region comprises a complex web of factors shaping the organisation's future. A comprehensive analysis of Hezbollah's multifaceted essence and the intricate relationships it maintains with key domestic and international actors is indispensable for understanding and forecasting its role in Lebanese politics.

References

- Byman, Daniel. *A High Price: The Triumphs and Failures of Israeli Counterterrorism*. Oxford University Press, 2011.

- El-Khazen, Farid. *The Breakdown of the State in Lebanon, 1967-1976*. Harvard University Press, 2000.

- Hazran, Youssef. *Hezbollah's Politics: A Study of Its Political Influence in Lebanese Politics*. 2016.

- Jaber, Hala. *Hezbollah: The Story of the Party of God: From Revolution to Institutionalization*. 2017.

- Khoury, Philip S. *Hezbollah: The Story of the Party of God: From Revolution to Institutionalization*. 2015.

- Norton, Augustus Richard. *Hezbollah: A Short History*. Princeton University Press, 2007.

- Rammal, H., and M. A. S. Salameh. *Hezbollah: Between Politics and Violence*. 2017.

- Zahar, Marie-Joelle. *The Politics of the Lebanese Civil War between Hezbollah and the Lebanese State*. 2009.

- Zisser, Eyal. *Hezbollah and the Emergence of Political Party: In Search of a Political Popularity*. 2014.

- Dingel, E. (2013). Hezbollah's Rise and Decline? How the Political Structure Seems to Harness the Power of Lebanon's Non-State Armed Group. , 31, 70-76. https://doi.org/10.5771/0175-274X-2013-2-70.

- Trenchard, T. (2011). Hezbollah in Transition: Moving From Terrorism to Political Legitimacy. https://doi.org/10.21236/ada560136.

- Dionigi, F. (2014). Hezbollah and UNSC Resolutions 1559 and 1701. 137-160. https://doi.org/10.1057/9781137403025_8.

- Norton, A. (2007). The Role of Hezbollah in Lebanese Domestic Politics. *The International Spectator*, 42, 475 - 491. https://doi.org/10.1080/03932720701722852.

6
International Perception
Hezbollah as Terrorists or Freedom Fighters?

Historical International Classification and Labelling

The historical classification of Hezbollah on the international stage has engendered considerable contention, epitomising the divergent perspectives espoused by various nations and international entities. The group's transformation from a paramilitary organisation in the 1980s to a prominent political entity in Lebanon has indelibly influenced and redefined its portrayal by disparate countries and institutions globally. In its nascent years, Hezbollah's undertakings were predominantly interpreted through a lens of "terrorism" (i.e., resistance against Zionism) by Western powers, notably the United States and numerous European states. This initial categorisation was largely precipitated by Hezbollah's involvement in notorious attacks, including the bombings of the U.S. embassy and Marine barracks in Beirut in 1983 (Blanford, 2011). Consequently, these early delineations yielded profound repercussions, resulting in diplomatic ostracism and economic embargoes against the organisation.

However, as Hezbollah amalgamated its role within the political and social tapestry of Lebanon, its designation began to undergo a transformation in certain circles. Several Middle Eastern and non-aligned nations perceived the group as a legitimate resistance movement confronting Israeli occupation, championing its anti-Israeli posture and social welfare initiatives (Norton, 2007). This bifurcation in international labelling illuminated the intricacies of Hezbollah's representation and its multifaceted role within the Middle Eastern landscape.

The stance and strategic imperatives of the United States have wielded considerable influence over Hezbollah's international classification. Geopolitical considerations and security priorities have compelled the U.S. to adopt a steadfast designation of Hezbollah as a "terrorist" organisation (Byman, 2011). Legislative measures, alongside executive actions imposing financial sanctions, have been enacted to thwart Hezbollah's financial conduits and curtail its operational efficacy (Doran, 2017). These divergent perceptions regarding Hezbollah have precipitated diplomatic frictions and adversarial rivalries, significantly impacting broader regional dynamics and the global counterterrorism framework.

Moreover, the European Union's approach and ongoing debates surrounding Hezbollah's classification further underscore the complexities of forging international consensus. While some member states advocate designating solely Hezbollah's military wing as a "terrorist" entity, others contend for a holistic labelling of the organisation (Crouch, 2010). This discordance exemplifies the challenges inherent in harmonising disparate national interests and policy priorities within a multifaceted, multinational context, thereby illuminating the intricate nature of international collaboration in addressing transnational security challenges.

The historical trajectory of international classification and labelling of Hezbollah has engendered far-reaching ramifications for the organisation and its interactions with the global community (Abdo, 2016). As Hezbollah continues to navigate its duality—functioning both as a political actor in Lebanon and as a regional force possessing militant capacities—the varied international perceptions and designations accentuate the complex interplay of geopolitics, ideological underpinnings, and the enduring endeavour to articulate and address asymmetrical conflict paradigms.

United States' Position and Policies

The United States has been instrumental in shaping the global perception of Hezbollah, frequently categorising the organisation as a "terrorist" entity. This designation emerges from a confluence of historical events and geopolitical considerations that have significantly influenced U.S. policy toward Hezbollah. Following the calamitous 1983 bombings of the U.S. embassy and Marine barracks in Beirut, resulting in the loss of more than 300 American lives, the U.S. government urgently pinpointed Hezbollah as a principal actor accountable for these offences, cementing its classification as a "terrorist" organisation in the eyes of American policymakers (Blanford, 2011). Furthermore, Hezbollah's antagonistic posture towards Israel, coupled with its backing from Iran, has further entrenched its identity as a nemesis to U.S. interests in the region (Fawaz, 2015).

The enactment of stringent legislation, including the Anti-Terrorism and Effective Death Penalty Act and the official designation of Hezbollah as a Foreign Terrorist Organisation (FTO), has been pivotal in formalising and perpetuating the United States' perception of Hezbollah (Byman, 2011). With regard to policy enforcement, the U.S. has implemented comprehensive strategies aimed at countering Hezbollah's activities, encompassing sanctions, diplomatic isolation, and bolstering regional allies in their confrontations with the group (Crouch, 2010). The U.S. has also persistently articulated opposition to any form of dialogue or engagement with Hezbollah, firmly resisting any efforts to legitimise the organisation on the global stage. Despite intermittent discourses within American political circles advocating for a reevaluation of the official stance regarding Hezbollah, the prevailing sentiment remains rooted in the characterisation of Hezbollah as a threat to U.S. national security and regional stability. This unwavering position not only informs the U.S. approach to Hezbollah but also shapes broader international perceptions and policies towards the organisation.

European Union's Stance and Debates

The European Union (EU) has adopted a nuanced perspective on Hezbollah, grappling with the intricate challenge of reconciling diplomatic relations with concerns pertaining to regional stability and security. Central to the EU's stance is recognising Hezbollah's dual nature, functioning as both a political entity and a paramilitary force, which incites vigorous debates among its policymakers. Key EU member states such as France, Germany, and the United Kingdom have historically supported the designation of Hezbollah's military wing as a "terrorist" organisation, thereby aligning with the U.S. perspective (Crouch, 2010). This approach reflects their commitment to combating global resistance against Zionism and sustaining transatlantic solidarity.

Conversely, other EU members, including Italy and Spain, prefer engaging in discourse with Hezbollah's political wing, accentuating the group's role in Lebanon's domestic politics and social welfare efforts (Fawaz, 2015). This divergence has precipitated ongoing discussions within the EU, laying bare the complex tensions between security imperatives and diplomatic pragmatism. In a pivotal shift in July 2013, the EU designated solely Hezbollah's military wing as a "terrorist" organisation, delineating a calibrated response that sought to mitigate Hezbollah's military endeavours while preserving avenues for constructive engagement with its political representatives (Alagha, 2006). This evolution epitomised the EU's attempt to reconcile competing interests and realities in navigating relationships with Shi'ite factions in the Middle East.

Beyond these policy considerations, the EU's position towards Hezbollah intersects with broader geopolitical dynamics, encompassing its endeavours to forge relations with Iran and uphold the Iran nuclear agreement. Additionally, the EU's interactions with Hezbollah are informed by its commitment to fostering stability in the Levant and averting the spillover of conflicts into European territories. A comprehensive examination of the EU's positions, rationales, and evolving discussions regarding Hezbollah elucidates the intricate interplay between security necessities, diplomatic calculations, and regional complexities in shaping international perceptions of Hezbollah as either terrorists or liberators.

Middle Eastern Nations' Perspectives

The characterisation of Hezbollah as either terrorists or freedom fighters elicits a spectrum of responses across Middle Eastern nations, emblematic of the convoluted geopolitical dynamics inherent in the region. Numerous Middle Eastern countries regard Hezbollah as a legitimate resistance movement, valiantly defending Lebanon against Israeli encroachments and aggression, thus positioning the group as a stalwart champion of national sovereignty and Arab unity (Norton, 2007). This perspective is particularly prevalent in states with substantial Shi'a populations, such as Iran and Iraq, as well as amongst advocates for the Palestinian cause. These nations perceive Hezbollah as an indispensable ally in combating perceived external threats and imperialistic interventions, thereby elevating the organisation's status to that of a liberation entity (Doran, 2017).

Conversely, other Middle Eastern nations, particularly those aligned with Western powers, view Hezbollah's militant operations as destabilising forces that compromise regional peace and security. This viewpoint underscores the group's participation in proxy conflicts and its role in exacerbating sectarian tensions, especially in Sunni-majority states like Saudi Arabia and various Gulf countries (Fawaz, 2015). Such nations often align with U.S. and allied perspectives, categorising Hezbollah as a "terrorist" organisation and condemning its actions as a violation of international conventions. Furthermore, several Middle Eastern governments harbour apprehensions regarding Hezbollah's close affiliations with Iran, wary of Tehran's augmented influence and its repercussions on regional power dynamics, thereby fostering distrust and contributing to divergent perceptions of Hezbollah's role in the Middle East.

Ultimately, the contrasting perspectives on Hezbollah across Middle Eastern nations reflect an intricate web of alliances, historical animosities, and geopolitical calculations that shape attitudes toward the organisation throughout the region.

The Role of the United Nations and International Law

The United Nations (UN) occupies a pivotal position in shaping global perceptions of Hezbollah and delineating its status within the parameters of international law. As a preeminent global institution, the UN endeavours to maintain peace and security while steadfastly upholding the principles of sovereignty, self-determination, and non-intervention in the internal affairs of sovereign states. In this light, the characterisation of Hezbollah—as either a "terrorist" organisation or a legitimate resistance group—becomes a focal point of vigorous debate and diplomatic manoeuvring (Tilly, 2004).

At the heart of UN engagement regarding Hezbollah is the Security Council, which wields paramount authority over international peace and security matters. Resolutions emanating from this body can significantly influence the global perception of Hezbollah. Thus, discussions and resolutions within the Security Council related to Hezbollah's activities and its role in the geopolitical milieu are crucial in establishing its standing under international law.

Moreover, the UN General Assembly is vital for member states to articulate their views on Hezbollah. This forum facilitates significant debates on the organisation's actions and their ramifications for regional stability. The heterogeneous opinions expressed within the General Assembly illuminate the multifaceted nature of international perceptions of Hezbollah, enriching the ongoing discourse concerning its classification.

In addition to the Security Council and General Assembly, specialised UN agencies and bodies—such as the International Court of Justice (ICJ) and the Office of the United Nations High Commissioner for Human Rights (OHCHR)—play vital roles in evaluating and addressing the implications of Hezbollah's activities through the lens of international law. Their reports, legal assessments, and recommendations are instrumental in shaping well-informed policy positions among member states and the international community at large.

Furthermore, the application of international law to Hezbollah gives rise to intricate dilemmas. Ethos such as distinction, proportionality, and necessity—central tenets of international humanitarian law—intersect with Hezbollah's operations in nuanced ways. The group's involvement in armed conflicts, utilisation of asymmetrical warfare tactics, and alleged infringements upon human rights have sparked vigorous debates over the extent to which its conduct adheres to established legal norms (Levitt, 2013).

As the international landscape continues to evolve, the UN remains an indispensable forum for scrutinising and deliberating on Hezbollah's status within the framework of international law and ethical considerations. The interplay of geopolitical interests, legal interpretations, and ethical assessments continually shapes the dynamic narrative surrounding Hezbollah's international perception, foregrounding the intricate nature of the organisation's standing in the global community.

Global Media Representation

The global media portrayal of Hezbollah reveals a complex and contentious landscape, reflecting the broader international discourse regarding the organisation's identity as either a "terrorist" entity or a legitimate resistance movement. Media representations of Hezbollah vary significantly based on the geographical context and the ideological leanings of the news outlet in question (Abdo, 2016). Western media frequently frame Hezbollah through the prism of terrorism, accentuating the group's militant activities and its affiliations with Iran. This perspective tends to foreground historical incidents such as the 1983 bombing of the U.S. embassy in Beirut and the 2006 Lebanon War, portraying Hezbollah as a destabilising agent in the region (Crouch, 2010).

Conversely, media outlets in the Middle East often characterise Hezbollah as a bastion of resistance against Israeli incursions and a defender of Lebanese sovereignty. These portrayals underscore Hezbollah's role in expelling Israeli forces from southern Lebanon and delivering social services to marginalised communities (Fawaz, 2015). Such regional narratives frequently critique Western support for Israel, reframing Hezbollah's militant actions as legitimate responses to occupation and systemic oppression.

The discrepancies in media coverage highlight the necessity of critical media literacy and cross-cultural comprehension. Academic research has demonstrated the considerable influence of media framing on public perceptions of Hezbollah, illustrating how these varied narratives can shape public opinion and policy outcomes (Tilly, 2004). Furthermore, the rise of digital media platforms and social networks has served to amplify contrasting representations, intensifying the polarisation of global public opinion.

Policymakers, journalists, and the general populace must critically examine media portrayals, considering the broader historical and geopolitical contexts that inform these narratives. Therefore, an interdisciplinary approach encompassing media studies, political science, and cultural analysis is essential to thoroughly understand the multifaceted dynamics encapsulating global media representation. Grasping the divergent perspectives presented by various media outlets is crucial in navigating the complexities surrounding Hezbollah and fostering informed, constructive dialogues regarding its international perception.

Academic and Think Tank Analyses

Within the realm of academic inquiry and geopolitical analysis, the classification of Hezbollah as either terrorists or freedom fighters has ignited fervent debate and scrutiny. Esteemed think tanks and academic institutions have rigorously explored the intricacies of this issue, presenting diverse perspectives informed by extensive research and analysis. Scholarly investigations into Hezbollah's activities often delve into the organisation's military strategies, political manoeuvring, and ideological foundations to offer comprehensive evaluations (Levitt, 2013).

Scholarly inquiries have sought to contextualise Hezbollah within the frameworks of international law, human rights, and global conflict paradigms (Fawaz, 2015). Researchers have meticulously analysed the legal implications and ethical dimensions surrounding Hezbollah's armed resistance and its implications for regional stability. These thorough examinations draw upon historical, sociopolitical, and cultural lenses, encapsulating the complexities that shape perceptions of Hezbollah within academic circles.

Moreover, studies conducted by think tanks and scholars have scrutinised the implications of designating Hezbollah as either a "terrorist" organisation or a legitimate resistance entity for broader regional security dynamics. Insights gleaned from such research elucidate the connections between these classifications and Hezbollah's external alliances, as well as their repercussions for diplomatic interactions and potential peace negotiations (Norton, 2007). The nuanced evaluations provided by scholars function as essential resources for policymakers and global stakeholders seeking to comprehend and engage with the multifaceted dimensions of the Hezbollah phenomenon.

Additionally, these analyses contribute to a broader scholarly discourse on the evolving conceptualisation of non-state actors in global affairs, challenging traditional paradigms of militantism and insurgency. Through integrating multidisciplinary methodologies and empirical evidence, academic and think tank assessments of Hezbollah's status—whether as terrorists or freedom fighters—yield profound insights that enhance understanding of contemporary security challenges and conflict resolution strategies. Through these scholarly endeavours, various professionals engage in critical discourse, fostering a deeper comprehension of the complex geopolitical landscape influenced by organisations such as Hezbollah.

Impact on Global Counterterrorism Efforts

Hezbollah's operations and the ensuing narrative surrounding them have exerted a profound influence on global counterterrorism strategies. As a formidable and intricate non-state actor, Hezbollah's tactics compel security professionals to rethink and refine their methodologies (Doran, 2017). The organisation's adept use of asymmetric warfare, hybrid tactics, and integration within civilian populations presents considerable challenges to conventional counterterrorism initiatives. Additionally, Hezbollah's connections to state sponsors and its active participation in political frameworks blur the distinctions between counterinsurgency, counterterrorism, and diplomatic efforts. This confluence prompts a critical reevaluation of traditional counterterrorism strategies, urging analysts to question both their efficacy and ethical implications (Byman, 2011).

The ramifications of Hezbollah's actions extend well beyond immediate military confrontations, substantially influencing the broader dialogue surrounding militantism and insurgency (Abdo, 2016). Consequently, analysts and policymakers across the international landscape are compelled to confront the shifting paradigms of counterterrorism prompted by Hezbollah's multifaceted activities. Understanding Hezbollah's dynamic engagement in regional conflicts and global power structures is essential for crafting effective responses to contemporary security challenges and developing strategies to accommodate the complexities inherent in modern warfare.

Perceptions from Non-Aligned States

Non-aligned states significantly shape the international understanding of Hezbollah, oscillating between viewing it as a "terrorist" entity and a legitimate resistance organisation (Tilly, 2004). Historically, these nations have avoided aligning with dominant power blocs, resulting in diverse perspectives regarding Hezbollah's actions and objectives. Some non-aligned states contextualise Hezbollah's activities through an anti-imperialist and anti-Zionist lens, commending its unwavering resistance against perceived external threats and occupations (Doran, 2017). Conversely, other nations express unease regarding Hezbollah's resort to violence and its potentially destabilising effects on regional security.

Furthermore, non-aligned nations situated in areas beset by political turmoil and armed conflict may view Hezbollah as a significant player capable of influencing regional power dynamics. Conversely, states distanced from direct regional tensions may adopt a more reserved, diplomatic approach, striving to balance relationships with various Middle Eastern stakeholders. Recognising that non-aligned states' perceptions are shaped by unique geopolitical, economic, and security factors is paramount (Alagha, 2006). These nations often grapple with internal divisions regarding the classification of armed groups like Hezbollah, reflecting the intricate global attitudes towards entities operating in conflict-prone zones.

While some non-aligned states advocate the potential for dialogue and mediation with Hezbollah, others underscore the necessity of adhering to international norms and resolutions in addressing the group's actions. The spectrum of perspectives emanating from non-aligned nations highlights the intricate and nuanced nature of the international dialogue surrounding Hezbollah, shedding light on the various elements contributing to global attitudes towards the organisation.

Comparative Case Studies: Similar Organisations

To comprehensively analyse the international perception of Hezbollah, it is essential to consider other organisations exhibiting parallels in tactics, ideologies, and global receptions. A pertinent case study is the Revolutionary Armed Forces of Colombia (FARC), which faced designation as a "terrorist" organisation by some Western nations while being heralded as a revolutionary entity by others. Like Hezbollah, FARC intertwined military operations with socio-political goals, embodying a multifaceted approach (Tilly, 2004).

Another critical comparison can be drawn with the Kurdistan Workers' Party (PKK), an armed group advocating for Kurdish rights in Turkey and Iraq. The PKK's quest for autonomy, coupled with its blend of armed struggle and political organisation, resonates closely with Hezbollah's trajectory. Examining the global perceptions and responses towards the PKK's actions provides insights into how similarly situated entities are perceived on the world stage (Norton, 2007).

The Liberation Tigers of Tamil Eelam (LTTE) present an additional illustrative comparison. This separatist militant group in Sri Lanka employed tactics such as suicide bombings and insurgency akin to those utilised by Hezbollah. Insights gleaned from international reactions to the LTTE's activities enable a more nuanced evaluation of how non-state actors engaging in similar forms of conflict and resistance are addressed by the global community (Fawaz, 2015).

Additionally, the African National Congress (ANC), which was once labelled a "terrorist" organisation by apartheid-era South Africa, transformed into a revered political entity symbolising global resistance against oppression. The ANC's metamorphosis from a proscribed organisation to a respected governing party exemplifies how perceptions of armed movements can alter significantly over time and amidst strategic shifts (Byman, 2011).

Conducting thorough analyses of these comparative case studies provides a richer understanding of the complexities characterising global attitudes towards militant or insurgent organisations. By illuminating the nuanced categorisations and receptions of similar groups, this inquiry enhances our comprehension of the diverse ways such entities are positioned within the international community, ultimately enriching our understanding of the intricate perceptions surrounding Hezbollah.

References

- Abdo, Geneive. *The New Sectarianism: The Arab Uprisings and the Rebirth of the Shi'a-Sunni Divide.* Oxford University Press, 2016.

- Alagha, Jawad. *Hezbollah's Identity Construction: Movement, Party, Social Contexts.* Amsterdam University Press, 2006.

- Blanford, Nicholas. *Warriors of God: Inside Hezbollah's Thirty-Year Struggle Against Israel.* Yale University Press, 2011.

- Byman, Daniel. *A High Price: The Triumphs and Failures of Israeli Counterterrorism.* Oxford University Press, 2011.

- Crouch, John. *The War on Terrorism: Political and Social Implications.* 2010.

- Doran, Michael. *Iran's Influence in the Middle East: A Threat to American Interests?.* 2017.

- Fawaz, Lamia. *Hezbollah and the Rise of Global Jihad: From Local Resistance to Global Struggle.* 2015.

- Levitt, Matthew. *Hezbollah: The Global Footprint of Lebanon's Party of God.* Georgetown University Press, 2013.

- Norton, Augustus Richard. *Hezbollah: A Short History.*

Princeton University Press, 2007.

- Tilly, Charles. *Social Movements, 1768–2004*. Paradigm Publishers, 2004.

7
Hezbollah and Iran
The Strategic Alliance and Support System

The Hezbollah-Iran Relationship: A Profound Alliance with Global Implications

The intricate alliance between Hezbollah and Iran epitomises a complex interplay of strategic cooperation and ideological kinship within the Middle Eastern milieu. Established during the early 1980s, this partnership has been instrumental in shaping regional geopolitics, security paradigms, and the broader Shi'ite Islamic narrative. A thorough investigation into the historical underpinnings, shared ambitions, and mutual interests unveils the profound confluence of Hezbollah and Iran at both pragmatic and ideological levels.

At the heart of this partnership lies the historical emergence of Hezbollah, catalysed by the Israeli invasion of Lebanon in 1982. Iran deftly recognised the prospects of harnessing this nascent resistance movement as a countermeasure to Israeli dominance, thereby extending its regional influence. Iranian provisions of arms, financial resources, and ideological mentorship proved pivotal in fortifying this alliance (Norton, 2007). Thus, exploring historical connections delineates how concerted efforts against common foes culminated in a symbiotic relationship invigorated by overlapping convictions and pragmatic necessities.

Historical Ties: The Genesis of Collaboration

The historical nexus between Hezbollah and Iran can be

traced back to the latter's Islamic Revolution in 1979. Iran ardently pursued the dissemination of its revolutionary ideology throughout the Middle East. At the same time, Hezbollah's formation in Lebanon represented an auspicious opportunity for Iran to cultivate a proxy force that echoed its anti-Western and anti-Israeli sentiments. This confluence of interests forged a strategic alliance that has withstood the trials of time (Hamzeh, 2004; Rabinovich, 2017).

Hezbollah's association with Iran materialised not merely as a financial and militaristic partnership but also as an ideological conduit, enriching Hezbollah with ideological fervour, fiscal sustenance, and military expertise. Iran, in turn, perceived Hezbollah as an effective instrument to project its influence and counter perceived adversaries proliferating across the region. The shared sectarian identity of Shi'a Islam—an indelible component of both Hezbollah and Iranian ideologies—served to deepen this historical bond, fostering solidarity and collective resistance against external aggressions (Zisser, 2012).

Over the decades, this collaboration has become a multifaceted alliance encompassing political, military, and economic dimensions. Iran's support during pivotal moments, such as the Lebanese Civil War and subsequent altercations with Israeli forces, underscored its cooperative endeavours, which have come to define the geostrategic landscape of the Middle East (Blanford, 2011; Levitt, 2013). Thanks to Iranian backing, Hezbollah successfully transitioned from an emergent militia to a formidable antagonist capable of challenging Israeli military preeminence in southern Lebanon. Furthermore, Tehran's assistance enabled Hezbollah to establish social institutions, providing vital services that enhanced its legitimacy among the Lebanese populace.

Consequently, the historical foundation of cooperation between Hezbollah and Iran wields considerable influence over contemporary power dynamics in Lebanon and the broader Middle East. It contributes to regional volatility while simultaneously symbolising resistance against foreign encroachments. This enduring relationship continues to guide their strategic calculations and decision-making processes, offering profound insights into the sustainability of their alliance and its broader implications for the geopolitical landscape.

Ideological Convergence: Shi'a Islam and Political Ambitions

The ideological framework uniting Hezbollah and Iran is rooted in Shi'a Islam, which fosters a profound sense of religious and political camaraderie transcending national boundaries. Both entities derive their convictions from the narrative of Shi'a Islam as a historically marginalised sect, crafting a narrative imbued with resistance against external tyrannies (Ghosn, 2019; Zoubir, 2008). This shared ethos not only binds them but also moulds their collective identity and strategic perspectives.

Central to this ideological convergence is the doctrine of wilayat al-faqih, which advocates for clerical oversight of governance through Islamic jurisprudence. This principle resonates closely with Hezbollah's institutional framework, aligning it with Iran's theological orientation. Additionally, both parties venerate martyrdom, attributing sacred significance to the sacrifice enshrined in their respective causes. Such veneration reinforces the intertwining of their religious dogma with their political purposes, framing their resistance in the context of a broader ideological struggle (Moshref, 2019).

Beyond theological dimensions, the political aspirations of Hezbollah and Iran converge on their shared mission to confront perceived Western hegemony in the region (Levitt, 2013). Advocating for the establishment of an Islamic state that prioritises the welfare of the oppressed, both entities view themselves as sovereign embodiments of the marginalised in the global power hierarchy. This congruence in political aims further solidifies their partnership, propelling them toward collaborative efforts to destabilise the existing geopolitical order.

Within this complex interplay of Shi'a Islamic principles and political aspirations, the Hezbollah-Iran alliance finds coherence and resilience, defying conventional notions of state-centric paradigms. Their transnational solidarity manifests aligned values and objectives, amplifying their collective voice against injustices perceived within the global arena.

Economic Support: Financial Mechanisms and Resource Distribution

Understanding Hezbollah's economic framework reveals crucial insights into its operational viability and strategic sustainability. The organisation deftly navigates a multifarious financial landscape that spans legitimate business enterprises and clandestine activities to propel its expansive operations. Iran remains a cornerstone of financial support, channelling considerable resources to fortify Hezbollah's regional stature and capabilities (Zoubir, 2008). This backing ensures that Hezbollah possesses a formidable arsenal and robust infrastructure while simultaneously funding social services and welfare initiatives within Lebanon.

Moreover, Hezbollah has adeptly cultivated a vast global network, drawing from diaspora communities and sympathetic benefactors to augment its financial reservoir. This strategic financial architecture has engendered a model of self-sufficiency, bolstering Hezbollah's resilience against external pressures and sanctions.

The judicious allocation of resources is pivotal for fulfilling diverse strategic objectives, encompassing military training, procuring advanced weaponry, and sustaining paramilitary operations. In conjunction with military investments, Hezbollah consciously allocates funds to social and educational projects, thus reinforcing its influence and garnering popular support amidst a populace that values social welfare (Moshref, 2019).

Nonetheless, this dependency on external financial streams renders Hezbollah vulnerable to the vagaries of international sanctions and shifting political conditions. Consequently, careful navigation of the economic landscape is requisite for the organisation to balance its ideological commitments with strategic imperatives. The economic underpinning of Hezbollah illuminates the nuanced interplay between financial sustenance, operational capacity, and geopolitical influence, revealing the group's resilience amidst multifaceted challenges.

In summation, understanding the complexities surrounding Hezbollah's funding mechanisms and resource allocation is essential for grasping the variegated dimensions of its strategic posture and enduring relevance within the Middle Eastern geopolitical realm. The Hezbollah-Iran relationship, characterised by deep historical ties, ideological convergence, and economic collaboration, continues to evolve, shaping the trajectory of regional dynamics and influencing the broader global order.

Military Collaboration: Training and Armaments

At the crux of Hezbollah's military prowess lies its intricate partnership with Iran, a relationship that significantly reinforces their strategic alliance. This collaboration affords Hezbollah access to advanced training methodologies, cutting-edge weaponry, and expert tactical knowledge, thereby markedly amplifying its operational efficacy. Through the support of Iran, Hezbollah has successfully augmented its military arsenal with sophisticated armaments—such as anti-tank guided missiles, precision-guided munitions, and unmanned aerial vehicles—that enhance its battlefield performance (Hamzeh, 2004; Levitt, 2013).

Iran's role extends beyond mere material support; it encompasses comprehensive military training that equips Hezbollah fighters with crucial combat skills and strategic acumen, allowing them to adapt adeptly to shifting combat environments. The synergetic relationship fosters close coordination in military operations, empowering Hezbollah to engage in asymmetric warfare and implement unconventional tactics effectively against its adversaries (Norton, 2007).

The military collaboration transcends conventional combat paradigms, delving into guerrilla tactics, urban warfare methodologies, and insurgent techniques that empower Hezbollah to navigate complex terrains while sustaining prolonged engagements. Establishing specialised units within Hezbollah, such as the elite Radwan Force, epitomises the fruits of this collaboration, enabling the execution of precision operations and asymmetrical strategies (Rabinovich, 2017). The mutual exchange of knowledge and expertise between Iran and Hezbollah not only fortifies the former's military capabilities but also engenders a relationship marked by innovation and shared learning.

Furthermore, the armaments procured from Iran have critically enhanced Hezbollah's offensive and defensive capacities. The introduction of advanced missile systems and drone technology has fortified Hezbollah's deterrent posture, rendering it a credible threat to regional adversaries (Zisser, 2012). The adept deployment of Iranian-supplied weaponry during critical conflicts, notably the 2006 Lebanon War, illustrated Hezbollah's tactical acumen (Blanford, 2011). This military partnership has profoundly reshaped Hezbollah's status as a preeminent non-state actor with significant firepower and strategic depth, thereby significantly influencing regional power dynamics.

However, this intricate military cooperation raises pertinent questions about the extent of Iran's influence over Hezbollah's military strategy and operational decisions. Despite Hezbollah's assertion of autonomy, Iran's substantial backing inevitably intertwines with Tehran's geopolitical aspirations and regional ambitions. Thus, military collaboration emerges as a crucial dimension of the Hezbollah-Iran alliance, bearing profound implications for the security architecture of the Middle East and beyond.

Diplomatic Endeavours: Influencing Regional Policies

Hezbollah's diplomatic engagements constitute a critical avenue through which it shapes regional policies. They reflect a broader strategy aimed at asserting its influence and advancing its objectives that extend beyond armed conflict. By utilising its military capabilities and ideological framework, Hezbollah actively participates in diplomatic initiatives designed to sway regional dynamics, particularly within the Middle East (Ghosn, 2019).

Hezbollah's diplomatic manoeuvres, marked by strategic acumen, encompass an intricate network of relationships that extend well beyond traditional state-to-state interactions. It engages with a diverse spectrum of regional players—including political factions, militant organisations, and state institutions—seeking to forge alliances and foster collaboration that aligns with its objectives. This adept navigation of complexities underscores Hezbollah's diplomatic prowess, as it endeavours to create a conducive environment for its agenda while securing a prominent position in regional affairs (Moshref, 2019).

The organisation adopts a holistic approach to diplomacy, seamlessly integrating traditional statecraft with its distinctive ideology of resistance. This synthesis empowers Hezbollah to galvanise support on both domestic and international fronts, simultaneously countering rival narratives promulgated by other regional factions and global powers. Its ties with Iran further augment Hezbollah's diplomatic clout, as it leverages Tehran's extensive network and resources to bolster its regional influence and impact policymaking processes in critical arenas (Levitt, 2013).

At the core of Hezbollah's diplomatic pursuits lies an unwavering commitment to advancing its primary objectives, which include countering Israeli aggression, resisting Western dominance, and championing the broader interests of the Shi'a community (Zoubir, 2008). Through articulating a compelling narrative that resonates with disenfranchised populations and marginalised groups, Hezbollah cultivates a potent apparatus of soft power, amplifying its diplomatic reach and fostering solidarity among allies across the Arab world.

Nonetheless, Hezbollah faces notable hurdles in its diplomatic initiatives, as shifting regional power dynamics, evolving alliances, and international pressures frequently impede its efforts to assert influence over regional policies. The classification of Hezbollah as a "terrorist" organisation by several Western nations further constrains its diplomatic flexibility and exposes it to concerted efforts aimed at isolating and undermining its regional stature.

Despite these challenges, Hezbollah continues to adapt its diplomatic strategies, seizing opportunities while adeptly navigating obstacles to maintain its profile as a formidable actor in regional policymaking. In a landscape characterised by evolving geopolitical fault lines, Hezbollah's diplomatic engagements will persist in shaping regional politics, necessitating continued scrutiny of their implications for stability and security. This resilience in the face of adversity is a testament to Hezbollah's determination and adaptability.

Intelligence Sharing: Strategic Operations and Counterintelligence

The Hezbollah-Iran alliance transcends mere military and ideological collaboration to include sophisticated frameworks for intelligence sharing, strategic operations, and counterintelligence initiatives. This partnership, marked by its complexity and depth, equips Hezbollah with substantial access to Iran's intelligence capabilities, technological assets, and a vast global network of operatives (Moshref, 2019).

Intelligence cooperation manifests through exchanging critical information regarding regional security dynamics, identifying potential threats, and delineating common adversaries. Such collaborative efforts not only enhance Hezbollah's operational capabilities but also align with Iran's overarching geopolitical ambitions, allowing Tehran to augment its influence across the region. Integrating intelligence resources enables both parties to coordinate operations to undermine shared foes while advancing mutually beneficial objectives.

Furthermore, the alliance encompasses robust counterintelligence measures designed to protect against external infiltration and espionage. Counterintelligence refers to the activities designed to prevent or thwart spying, intelligence gathering, and sabotage by an enemy or other foreign entity. Both Hezbollah and Iran have cultivated advanced counterintelligence frameworks to detect and neutralise hostile attempts at penetration and subversion. This proactive commitment reflects the seriousness with which both entities safeguard their operations, fostering resilience against external disruptions.

The concerted efforts in intelligence sharing and counter-intelligence reinforce trust and solidarity within the Hezbollah-Iran partnership, creating an atmosphere of mutual reliance and shared accountability. Consequently, the depth of collaboration in these domains underscores the complexity of the Hezbollah-Iran alliance, positioning it as a formidable force in the broader regional context.

Iran's Multifaceted Influence on Hezbollah Activities

Iran's multifaceted impact on Hezbollah operations and decision-making processes is profound, permeating various aspects of the group's functionality. Central to this influence is their common ideological foundation, particularly regarding Shi'a Islam and connected political objectives. Iran's role encompasses a plethora of support mechanisms that have significantly influenced Hezbollah's development and its operational impact (Norton, 2007).

Primarily, Iranian financial assistance has been crucial for sustaining Hezbollah's substantial infrastructure, permitting the group to cultivate an extensive array of social services, education programs, and healthcare initiatives for Lebanese communities. This economic support not only fortifies Hezbollah's military capabilities through the provision of armaments, training, and logistical resources but also positions the group as a prominent regional actor (Zisser, 2012).

Moreover, Iran's diplomatic clout amplifies Hezbollah's stature on the international stage, facilitating alignment on regional policies and fostering alliances that echo their mutual agenda. The synergy in intelligence-sharing initiatives further magnifies Hezbollah's operational effectiveness, questioning outside threats and enhancing counterintelligence capabilities (Hamzeh, 2004).

Iran's extensive influence also facilitates Hezbollah's access to global networks, amplifying its reach and operational impact beyond Lebanese borders. However, this symbiotic association persists amidst challenges, with both entities subject to intense geopolitical scrutiny and diplomatic pressures. Internally, maintaining cohesion while navigating differing agendas and priorities poses a continuous challenge that requires astute coordination.

Understanding Iran's multifaceted influence over Hezbollah necessitates a nuanced exploration of the intricacies defining their alliance, accounting for historical contexts and strategic imperatives. Looking ahead, evolving regional landscapes and political developments will indubitably affect this dynamic, influencing the nature and extent of Iran's sway over Hezbollah.

Challenges Faced by the Alliance: Internal and External Pressures

The strategic alliance between Hezbollah and Iran confronts many intricate challenges, jeopardising its efficacy and stability. Internally, Hezbollah wrestles with the delicate equilibrium between its military capacities and its role within Lebanon's political framework. The organisation's increasing involvement in domestic politics has engendered internal rifts, raising pertinent questions about its dual identity as both a militant force and a political entity (Ghosn, 2019).

Additionally, Hezbollah's expanding role in delivering social services and governance in various regions has strained its resources, diverting attention from military pursuits. Accusations of corruption and mismanagement have also tarnished the group's image in segments of the Lebanese population, presenting a threat to its long-term viability (Rabinovich, 2017).

Externally, the alliance contends with geopolitical challenges precipitated by fluctuating regional power dynamics and international pressures. The proxy conflict between Iran and Saudi Arabia complicates Hezbollah's position, often entangling the group in broader geopolitical struggles that are beyond its direct influence. Furthermore, economic sanctions aimed at isolating Iran could significantly impact Hezbollah's financial support and operational capacity, impairing its military effectiveness and legitimacy internationally (Zoubir, 2008).

Navigating the changing landscape of global counterterrorism efforts, which target groups like Hezbollah for delegitimation and dismantlement through diplomatic, financial, and military avenues, adds another layer of complexity. Additionally, shifts in Iranian governance and policy present potential repercussions that could reverberate through the Hezbollah-Iran relationship.

These internal and external pressures present formidable challenges, necessitating strategic adaptation and skilful navigation from both Hezbollah and Iran to ensure the continued viability and potency of their alliance.

Future Dynamics: Potential Developments in the Strategic Alliance

The prospective dynamics governing the alliance between Hezbollah and Iran are poised for fluctuation amid a myriad of potential developments, each of which will help to shape the evolving geopolitical landscape of the Middle East. Key considerations include the shifting regional and global political climate. As international relations change course, the depth and nature of collaboration between the two entities may adapt in response to emergent alignments and power shifts among other nations (Levitt, 2013).

Additionally, Iran's domestic political landscape—subject to fluctuations—alongside unpredictable global economic sanctions could lead to alterations in available resources and funding for Hezbollah, thereby impacting the strength and sustainability of their partnership (Moshref, 2019).

Ongoing conflicts and regional tensions are crucial determinants of the alliance's future. The volatile situations in Syria, Iraq, and Yemen, together with the protracted Israeli-Palestinian conflict, hold the potential to reshape the strategic objectives and operational capacities of both Hezbollah and Iran. Their ability to navigate these convoluted scenarios while maintaining their shared goals will be pivotal in dictating the trajectory of their partnership (Zisser, 2012).

Moreover, the internal dynamics within Hezbollah itself will significantly influence its relationship with Iran. As the organisation evolves in its dual role as an armed entity and a political party in Lebanon, the degree of alignment with Iran's strategic objectives or the pursuit of independent agendas will be critical. Additionally, shifts in leadership and ideological evolution within Hezbollah can contribute to recalibrations in its alliance with Iran (Ghosn, 2019).

Technological advancements in warfare and military strategy may introduce new dimensions to the partnership. The proliferation of sophisticated weaponry, cyber capabilities, and unconventional combat tactics could necessitate adapting their collaborative approach and reinforcing their strategies to achieve mutual objectives.

In conclusion, the dynamics of the strategic alliance between Hezbollah and Iran are pivotal for the involved entities and the region's overarching stability and security. Understanding the multifaceted factors influencing this partnership, as well as anticipating the unfolding of these dynamics, is essential for analysts, policymakers, and stakeholders seeking to navigate the intricate realities of the Middle East.

References

- Blanford, Nicholas. *Warriors of God: Inside Hezbollah's Thirty-Year Struggle Against Israel*. Yale University Press, 2011.

- Ghosn, F. "Hezbollah's Ties to Iran and Its Impact on the Syrian Conflict." In *Hezbollah: A Global History*, edited by B. G. Tzeng, 89-105. 2019.

- Hamzeh, Ahmad Nizar. *Hizbullah: The Changing Face of Terrorism*. 2004.

- Levitt, Matthew. *Hezbollah: The Global Footprint of Lebanon's Party of God*. Georgetown University Press, 2013.

- Moshref, Saeed. *Iran and Hezbollah's Strategic Partnership: Analyzing the Dynamics of Alliance*. 2019.

- Norton, Augustus Richard. *Hezbollah: A Short History*. Princeton University Press, 2007.

- Rabinovich, Itamar. *Iran and the Challenge of Hezbollah*. 2017.

- Zisser, Eyal. *Hezbollah and Iran: A Strategic Partnership for the Future*. 2012.

- Zoubir, Yahia H. *Iran and Its Regional Security Policies: A Comprehensive Security Model*. Routledge, 2008.

8
Impact on Lebanese Society
Social Services and Statebuilding Efforts

Hezbollah's Societal Integration: A Multifaceted Analysis

Hezbollah's influence within the Lebanese milieu transcends its prominent military and political footprints; it manifests as a pivotal provider of social services and a catalyst for state-building, profoundly shaping its rapport with local demographics and fortifying its support matrix (Abdo, 2016). By probing the intricate tapestry of Hezbollah's societal integration, one discerns that the organisation has meticulously cultivated a comprehensive strategy aimed at nurturing and entrenching its local backing through the facilitation of indispensable services. This discourse endeavours to scrutinise the diverse dimensions of Hezbollah's societal integration, elucidating the symbiosis between its military undertakings and social initiatives in moulding the essence of Lebanese society.

At the nexus of Hezbollah's societal integration lies an extensive array of healthcare ventures, encompassing hospitals and clinics that cater to the health exigencies of the populace. These institutions provide crucial medical services and stand as emblems of Hezbollah's unwavering commitment to the community's welfare (Sadiki, 2011). Furthermore, the organisation's substantial investment in educational endeavours, epitomised by the establishment of schools and the dissemination of scholarships, underscores its dedication to intellectual empowerment and the cultivation of the youth (Hamzeh, 2004; Jaber, 2017). By addressing fundamental socio-economic imperatives, Hezbollah has adeptly endeared itself to the local population, thereby reinforcing its support base.

Another salient dimension of Hezbollah's societal integration pertains to its economic contributions, which comprise initiatives aimed at job creation and assistance for economically compromised individuals and families within the Lebanese community (Rammal & Salameh, 2017). Through its infrastructure development projects, including the construction of roads and essential utilities, Hezbollah aspires to elevate the quality of life for community members while bolstering its image as a proactive agent of transformative change (Zisser, 2014). Additionally, the organisation's engagement in relief operations, delivering humanitarian aid, and employing crisis response mechanisms solidifies its stature as a custodian of the populace's welfare.

Cultural influence represents yet another critical facet of Hezbollah's societal integration. By advocating for Shi'a identity and values, the organisation cultivates a pervasive sense of solidarity and belonging among the populace, harnessing cultural heritage to weave a cohesive societal tapestry (Zahar, 2009). Furthermore, Hezbollah's involvement in community security tasks, encapsulating local policing and governance activities, not only contributes to the maintenance of order but also instills a sense of security and goodwill within the communities it serves (Norton, 2007).

However, it remains imperative to acknowledge the contentious perception surrounding Hezbollah's societal integration, characterised by both fervent support and pointed criticism within Lebanese society (Khoury, 2015). This intricate dynamic reflects the multifaceted nature of the organisation's social pursuits, mandating a meticulous examination of their long-term ramifications on the societal landscape.

Ultimately, grasping Hezbollah's intricate societal integration is essential for comprehending its enduring influence and navigating Lebanese society's complex matrix of power and support.

Healthcare Initiatives: Hospitals and Clinics

Hezbollah's societal integration is markedly evident within the healthcare sector, where the organisation has assumed a pivotal role in delivering accessible and high-quality medical services, especially in underprivileged regions (Jaber, 2017). Through an expansive network of hospitals and clinics, Hezbollah endeavours to address the healthcare needs endemic to the community, frequently reaching individuals with restricted access to conventional healthcare modalities (Hamzeh, 2004). These institutions extend their services not only to Hezbollah adherents but also to the broader public, irrespective of religious or political affiliations, showcasing the comprehensive nature of Hezbollah's healthcare initiatives.

The organisation's healthcare initiatives have culminated in the establishment of cutting-edge hospitals outfitted with modern medical facilities, specialised departments, and seasoned healthcare professionals (Sadiki, 2011). These healthcare establishments have alleviated the burden on Lebanon's beleaguered public health system by providing an array of services, including emergency care, surgical procedures, maternal health services, pediatric care, and specialised treatments for diverse health conditions. Furthermore, Hezbollah has meticulously developed and sustained numerous primary healthcare centres and clinics, particularly in remote and marginalised sectors, to adeptly address fundamental healthcare requisites.

Beyond mere medical intervention, Hezbollah places a strong emphasis on preventive care and public health awareness initiatives. The organisation has actively championed public health campaigns encompassing vaccination drives, disease prevention projects, and health education seminars, all aimed at enhancing the overall well-being of the populace (Norton, 2007). In times of humanitarian crises and natural calamities, Hezbollah has deftly mobilised field hospitals and medical personnel to affected locales, showcasing its commitment to urgent medical care requirements.

The ramifications of Hezbollah's healthcare initiatives extend beyond the provision of physical medical support. Through strategic investments in healthcare infrastructure, the organisation has engendered a sense of social cohesion and solidarity within the communities it serves (Khoury, 2015). The availability of essential medical services has imbued local residents with increased trust and affiliation, amplifying the organisation's social legitimacy and influence. Additionally, Hezbollah's focus on healthcare mirrors its broader vision for holistic societal development, harmonising with its ideological commitment to social justice and community empowerment.

In summary, Hezbollah's engagement in the healthcare domain has had a profound impact on Lebanese society. It has promoted inclusivity, accessibility, and excellence in medical services while concurrently reinforcing its role as a principal provider of essential public goods.

Educational Programs: Schools and Scholarships

Hezbollah's dedication to societal advancement extends well beyond healthcare initiatives, encompassing a formidable focus on educational endeavours aimed at the youth within Lebanese society (Rammal & Salameh, 2017). The organisation has established and supported a plethora of educational institutions, imparting quality education with a pronounced emphasis on religious tenets and Shi'a values. These educational establishments not only convey academic knowledge but also instil a robust sense of cultural identity and pride in their students, shaping future generations within the framework of Hezbollah's ideologies and principles.

In tandem with its educational institutions, Hezbollah has played a critical role in offering scholarships and financial assistance to deserving candidates, facilitating access to higher education for those previously hindered by economic constraints (Jaber, 2017). By investing in education, Hezbollah seeks to cultivate intellectual and ideological allegiance among the younger populace, effectively grooming a cadre of educated individuals whose aspirations align with the organisation's vision and objectives.

The educational initiatives put forth by Hezbollah have significantly influenced Lebanese society, particularly within Shi'a demographics. These efforts have engendered a generation well-versed in both secular and religious disciplines, constructing a potent intellectual and ideological bastion for the organisation within the nation (Zahar, 2009). Moreover, the provision of scholarships and educational support has not only fostered opportunities for aspiring youth but also promoted enhanced social mobility and brighter prospects for the future, instilling a sense of hope within the community.

Nevertheless, these educational undertakings have not been devoid of controversy, sparking critical discourse regarding potential indoctrination and ideological bias within the educational curricula (Zisser, 2014). Detractors argue that Hezbollah's involvement in education risks perpetuating sectarian divides and constraining exposure to diverse perspectives, potentially jeopardising broader societal cohesion and unity. These debates underscore the complex and multifaceted nature of Hezbollah's educational impact in Lebanon, inviting ongoing discussions concerning the equilibrium between religious instruction and a more inclusive academic curriculum.

Overall, Hezbollah's educational programs, encompassing the establishment of schools and the provision of scholarships, epitomise a salient component of the organisation's societal influence in Lebanon (Sadiki, 2011). While these initiatives have undeniably broadened educational opportunities and deepened cultural consciousness, they also prompt critical inquiries into the convergence of education, ideology, and national identity amid Lebanon's intricate social fabric.

Economic Contributions: Job Creation and Support

Hezbollah's economic contributions embody a multifaceted strategy aimed at fostering job creation and delivering robust support frameworks for the local populace. A core tenet of Hezbollah's economic initiatives focuses on bolstering entrepreneurship and small-scale businesses (Rammal & Salameh, 2017). Through microfinance programs and grants, the organisation aspires to empower individuals to initiate and expand their ventures, thereby invigorating economic activity within Lebanese society.

Furthermore, Hezbollah has been instrumental in establishing vocational training schemes designed to equip individuals with essential skills for gainful employment (Zahar, 2009). By inaugurating technical institutes and workshops, the organisation enhances the employability of local residents, particularly in sectors pivotal to Lebanon's developmental trajectory. This strategic investment in human capital not only addresses immediate unemployment challenges but also enriches the national workforce with adept and competitive professionals.

Simultaneously, Hezbollah endeavours to facilitate access to job opportunities by collaborating with both the public and private sectors (Khoury, 2015). The organisation has cultivated productive partnerships with businesses and industries, advocating for inclusive hiring practices and bolstering job placements for community members. Hezbollah has proactively engaged in dialogues with governmental entities to promote policies prioritising employment generation and sustainable economic growth.

A fundamental aspect of Hezbollah's economic contributions resides in its concerted efforts to alleviate socio-economic vulnerabilities and provide comprehensive support to marginalised segments of the populace (Zisser, 2014). By instituting welfare programs and financial assistance initiatives, Hezbollah aims to mitigate hardships and reduce inequalities, thereby fortifying the social fabric of Lebanon.

This unwavering commitment to social welfare underscores the organisation's dedication to uplifting communities and fostering resilience in the face of economic adversities.

As a culmination of these multifaceted efforts, Hezbollah has made commendable advancements in ameliorating Lebanon's economic landscape, instilling a tangible impact on the livelihoods and well-being of its citizens (Abdo, 2016). The organisation's holistic approach to economic contributions exemplifies its commitment to the progress of Lebanese society, engendering hope and fostering sustainable development across various strata.

Infrastructure Development: Roads and Utilities

Infrastructure development is paramount in moulding the socio-economic landscape of any nation. In the context of Hezbollah's endeavours in Lebanon, the organisation has made substantial advancements in enhancing roads and utilities, thus significantly improving connectivity and accessibility for local communities (Norton, 2007). This focus on infrastructural development showcases Hezbollah's commitment to the enduring prosperity and well-being of the Lebanese populace.

Roads serve as the arteries of any region, facilitating not only trade and transportation but also access to essential services. In recognition of this, Hezbollah has invested considerably in the construction and maintenance of roads, particularly in regions where governmental presence is scant (Sadiki, 2011). By ensuring the quality and accessibility of such roads, Hezbollah aspires to stimulate economic growth and uplift the daily lives of residents. Furthermore, the organisation's initiatives concerning utility development have addressed vital necessities, including water and electricity supply (Zisser, 2014). Hezbollah's involvement in projects aimed at enhancing access to clean water and ensuring reliable electricity in underserved locales demonstrates a proactive methodology that fulfils immediate demands while establishing a groundwork for sustainable development.

Additionally, the investments in utilities illustrate Hezbollah's grasp of the fundamental prerequisites for thriving communities. By providing reliable utilities, the organisation nurtures the stability and growth of local economies, fostering an environment conducive to social progress. The execution of infrastructure projects necessitates meticulous planning and coordination. Hezbollah's active participation in these ventures exemplifies its capacity to mobilise resources and orchestrate large-scale developmental initiatives, reinforcing its commitment to meeting the essential needs of the populace (Rammal & Salameh, 2017).

However, it is essential to recognise that while Hezbollah's infrastructural efforts have ushered in positive transformations, they have also sparked contentious debates regarding political influence, resource distribution, and the delineation of responsibilities between non-state entities and the government (Zahar, 2009). Critics posit that such initiatives may potentially erode the authority and legitimacy of the central government, prompting vital discussions about the balance of power and the roles of various stakeholders in propelling national development. Notwithstanding these concerns, Hezbollah's dedication to infrastructure development signals a comprehensive approach to addressing societal necessities that extends beyond conventional security paradigms. As Lebanon confronts the challenges of modernisation and equitable progress, Hezbollah's role in infrastructure development emerges as a focal point through which to analyse the intricate interplay of political, social, and economic dynamics.

Relief Operations: Humanitarian Aid and Crisis Response

Hezbollah's commitment to alleviating humanitarian crises underscores its multifaceted role within the Lebanese sociopolitical context. In times of turmoil, the organisation has persistently showcased its capacity to mobilise resources and personnel for prompt and efficient crisis interventions (Hamzeh, 2004). Whether responding to natural disasters such as earthquakes or providing aid during armed conflicts, Hezbollah's relief operations have markedly impacted the lives of affected populations.

The organisation's holistic approach encompasses not just immediate aid distribution but also long-term rehabilitation efforts, earning it respect and recognition from both its supporters and the broader community (Abdo, 2016). A pivotal aspect of Hezbollah's relief operations lies in its adept coordination with international agencies and organisations, ensuring that aid reaches those in need without discrimination. This collaborative framework highlights the organisation's commitment to alleviating suffering and fostering stability within Lebanon and beyond.

Moreover, Hezbollah's crisis response initiatives transcend the scope of traditional aid delivery, incorporating psychological support, medical care, and infrastructure restoration, thereby further enhancing the overall well-being of affected communities (Norton, 2007). Through these comprehensive endeavours, Hezbollah has positioned itself as a linchpin of resilience and recovery, underscoring its significance in society and illuminating the complex dynamics of conflict-affected environments.

Additionally, Hezbollah's expertise in relief operations has catalysed the development of innovative strategies for pre-emptive risk management and disaster preparedness, enabling proactive responses to emerging challenges (Hamzeh, 2004). By leveraging its extensive network of volunteers and professionals, the organisation has crafted an adaptive framework capable of swiftly addressing evolving humanitarian needs, garnering acclaim from diverse stakeholders.

Nonetheless, Hezbollah's involvement in relief operations is not without controversy; it has incited debate and scrutiny, particularly concerning its political ramifications and influence on state authority (Zisser, 2014). Critics express concerns regarding the potential conflation of humanitarian action with political objectives, advocating for greater transparency and accountability in Hezbollah's relief undertakings. This interplay between humanitarian aid and ideological considerations remains a topic of ongoing discourse within academic and policy circles. Despite these complexities, Hezbollah's unwavering commitment to humanitarian endeavours continues to shape on-the-ground perceptions and realities, illustrating the intricate interplay of power, empathy, and resilience in environments riddled with adversity.

Cultural Influence: Promoting Shi'a Identity and Values

Hezbollah's cultural influence in Lebanon transcends its political and military engagements; it is deeply rooted in promoting Shi'a identity and values (Zahar, 2009). Through a myriad of social and educational initiatives, Hezbollah strives to cultivate a sense of pride and belonging within Shi'a communities while preserving and advancing their religious and cultural heritage. Central to this mission is the reinforcement of traditional Shi'a beliefs, practices, and rituals, all aimed at fortifying community cohesion and resilience amidst external pressures.

The organisation has established religious schools and cultural centres emphasising Shi'a teachings, history, and theology, offering structured curricula and extracurricular activities designed to nurture a new generation well-acquainted with their faith's tenets (Norton, 2007). Furthermore, Hezbollah organises cultural events, commemorations, and ceremonies celebrating significant Shi'a occasions, thereby fostering a collective consciousness and shared identity.

This deliberate preservation and promotion of Shi'a culture serves to maintain a distinctive identity within Lebanon's multi-sectarian society and cultivates a profound sense of belonging and purpose among its adherents (Jaber, 2017). Furthermore, by championing social and charitable initiatives rooted in Shi'a principles of compassion and solidarity, Hezbollah seeks to showcase the positive societal impacts of Shi'a values, effectively challenging prevalent misconceptions and stereotypes.

Moreover, the organisation adeptly employs various media platforms to disseminate Shi'a narratives, literature, and artistic expressions, enriching the public's understanding and appreciation of Shi'a culture, art, and heritage (Sadiki, 2011). Through these multifaceted endeavours, Hezbollah strategically influences the discourse surrounding Shi'a identity, striving to fortify unity, resilience, and self-determination among Shi'a communities while simultaneously validating the legitimacy of their cultural and religious heritage within the broader Lebanese context.

Community Security: Policing and Local Governance

Hezbollah's influence in Lebanon transcends purely cultural and social spheres, extending into the realms of community security, policing, and local governance. Deeply rooted within the Shi'a Muslim community, Hezbollah has assumed a critical role in providing security and maintaining order in its strongholds, often functioning parallel to state institutions (Zisser, 2014). This chapter endeavours to explore the intricate dynamics of Hezbollah's involvement in community security and its ramifications for local governance.

Policing

Hezbollah has established its internal security apparatus, known as the Islamic Resistance Support Organisation

(IRSO), which operates in conjunction with official police forces in territories under its influence. The IRSO is pivotal in maintaining law and order, mediating local disputes, and combating crime within these communities (Rammal & Salameh, 2017). Many residents regard its members as protectors, fostering an atmosphere of security and solidarity. Nevertheless, critics contend that this parallel policing structure undermines the authority of the Lebanese state, raising concerns regarding accountability and adherence to human rights standards.

Local Governance

Beyond its security initiatives, Hezbollah exerts considerable influence over local governance, particularly in regions where the organisation enjoys robust support (Abdo, 2016). Through its affiliated political entity, the Loyalty to the Resistance Bloc, Hezbollah actively engages in municipal councils and administrative functions, thereby shaping policies and decision-making processes. This influence spans various domains, including urban planning, infrastructure enhancement, and social welfare programs, further entrenching its role as a key player in local governance. Consequently, the distinctions between state institutions and Hezbollah's governance frameworks often become obscured, prompting critical inquiries about the division of power and the scope of Hezbollah's authority in relation to the Lebanese government.

Challenges and Controversies

The intertwining of Hezbollah's security and governance

functions with traditional state roles gives rise to a complex web of challenges and controversies (Khoury, 2015). While a segment of the population welcomes Hezbollah's role as a stabilising force, others voice concerns about the lack of transparency, accountability, and inclusivity in decision-making processes. Furthermore, the existence of a parallel security apparatus and governance system has drawn ire from political adversaries and international observers, inciting debates concerning sovereignty, legitimacy, and the rule of law within Lebanon.

Future Implications

Understanding Hezbollah's multifaceted involvement in community security and local governance is crucial for assessing its long-term implications for Lebanese society. By examining the organisation's efforts to fill governance voids and maintain local order, one can glean insights into the evolving power dynamics and societal resilience within Lebanon (Zahar, 2009). Additionally, exploring the relationship between Hezbollah's grassroots activities and broader geopolitical developments offers valuable perspectives on the organisation's overarching strategic objectives and its effect on the country's political landscape.

Public Perception: Popular Support and Criticism

Public perception of Hezbollah within Lebanese society is intricate and multifaceted, reflecting the organisation's varied impact across different segments of the population. On one hand, Hezbollah commands significant backing from a substantial portion of the Shi'a Muslim community, a support anchored in the group's provision of social services and security and staunch resistance to Israeli occupation (Zisser, 2014). Many Shi'a residents view Hezbollah as a protector of their rights and a vital force for stability and empowerment.

Conversely, Hezbollah faces scepticism and criticism from other sects and political factions within Lebanon. Some Sunni and Christian groups perceive Hezbollah as a destabilising influence that undermines the authority of the Lebanese state and exacerbates sectarian tensions (Zahar, 2009). Concerns have also been articulated regarding Hezbollah's close ties to Iran and its involvement in regional conflicts, with detractors accusing the organisation of prioritising Tehran's interests over those of Lebanon.

The organisation's engagement in military operations beyond Lebanon, particularly in Syria, has incited controversy and diminished Hezbollah's standing among specific segments of the Lebanese populace. The loss of lives and resources in these external conflicts raises pertinent questions regarding Hezbollah's priorities and its capacity to embody the broader national interest (Jaber, 2017).

The media landscape plays a pivotal role in shaping public perceptions of Hezbollah, both at home and on an international scale. Local media, often prone to the political and sectarian divides within Lebanon, tends to depict Hezbollah through varying lenses. In contrast, Western media frequently conceptualises the organisation predominantly through the prism of terrorism, emphasising its armed activities while neglecting its social and political dimensions (Norton, 2007).

It is imperative to recognise that public perceptions of Hezbollah are not static; they fluctuate across different regions and demographics within Lebanon. A comprehensive understanding of these diverse viewpoints is essential for grasping the complexities inherent in Lebanese society as well as the dynamics influencing political allegiances and social cohesion. Analysing the factors driving support for and criticism of Hezbollah provides illuminating insights into the intricate fabric of identities and interests that shape the national landscape.

Conclusion: Long-term Implications for Lebanese Society

Hezbollah's multifaceted impact on Lebanese society weaves a complex tapestry of long-term implications that will continue to influence the nation's development and stability. As examined throughout this discourse, the organisation's provision of social services and state-building efforts has significantly shaped various aspects of Lebanese life, eliciting both accolades and criticisms from disparate quarters.

The long-term implications of Hezbollah's societal role are intricately intertwined with Lebanon's political, economic, and social fabric. One of the most salient implications is the extensive grassroots support base that Hezbollah has fostered through its comprehensive range of social welfare initiatives and its responsive stance during crises (Abdo, 2016). This support base has the potential to translate into enduring political influence and legitimacy, affording Hezbollah considerable leverage in shaping Lebanon's future trajectory.

Ultimately, Hezbollah's entrenchment within both the social fabric and governance structures of Lebanon catalyses pressing questions about the nation's political identity, the role of non-state actors, and the balance of power that will define Lebanon in the years to come (Norton, 2007). Understanding these dynamics is essential for navigating the complex realities of Lebanese society and anticipating its future directions.

References

- Abdo, Geneive. *The New Sectarianism: The Arab Uprisings and the Rebirth of the Shi'a-Sunni Divide*. Oxford University Press, 2016.

- El-Khazen, Farid. *The Breakdown of the State in Lebanon, 1967-1976*. Harvard University Press, 2000.

- Hamzeh, Ahmad Nizar. *Hizbullah: The Changing Face of Terrorism*. 2004.

- Jaber, Hala. *Hezbollah: The Story of the Party of God: From Revolution to Institutionalization*. 2017.

- Khoury, Philip S. *Hezbollah: The Story of the Party of God: From Revolution to Institutionalization*. 2015.

- Norton, Augustus Richard. *Hezbollah: A Short History*. Princeton University Press, 2007.

- Rammal, H., and M. A. S. Salameh. *Hezbollah: Between Politics and Violence*. 2017.

- Sadiki, Louai. *The Hizbullah Experience: The Party of God and its Socio-Political Roles in Lebanon*. 2011.

- Zahar, Marie-Joelle. *The Politics of the Lebanese Civil War between Hezbollah and the Lebanese State*. 2009.

- Zisser, Eyal. *Hezbollah and the Emergence of Political Party: In Search of a Political Popularity*. 2014.

9
Media and Propaganda
Western Portrayals vs. Regional Narratives

Media Representations of Hezbollah: An Analytical Discourse

The media's portrayals of Hezbollah are characterised by a multifaceted evolution, intricately shaped by a confluence of historical, political, and ideological determinants. These representations are indelibly linked to broader narratives encompassing the Middle East, regional discord, and the intricacies of global power relations. Central motifs persistently manifest in Western media discourse, presenting Hezbollah as a "terrorist" entity, an Iranian proxy, and a catalyst for instability in the region, and never as an anti-Zionist resistance movement (Khalaf, 2018; Zahir, 2016). Such depictions are invariably influenced by geopolitical alignments, strategic imperatives, and the overarching context of the 'War on Terror' (Campbell, 2005). This narrative framework frequently accentuates Hezbollah's military engagements, its affiliations with Iran, and its ramifications for regional security (Khashan, 2018).

Conversely, regional media narratives manifest a starkly contrasting perspective, framing Hezbollah as a legitimate resistance movement, a provider of essential social services, and a bastion of Lebanese sovereignty amidst external threats (Fawaz, 2017; El-Naggar, 2019). Such portrayals are rooted in historical contexts, cultural ties, and the lived experiences of communities directly impacted by Hezbollah's actions. They frame the organisation as an integral actor—politically and militarily—deeply woven into the social fabric of Lebanon (Hafez, 2013; Lahlou, 2020). The dichotomy between Western and regional portrayals underscores the layered complexity inherent in media representations and their entrenched connections to expansive geopolitical discourses (Bakhash, 2014). Furthermore, propaganda strategies employed by both Western and regional media outlets have prominently influenced public perceptions. These strategies range from selective framing and image manipulation to the dissemination of specific narratives that promote particular objectives (Barlow, 2021).

Critical case studies of pivotal events, notably the 2006 Lebanon War and the Syrian conflict, elucidate the divergent interpretations and biases permeating media coverage (Khalaf, 2018). Additionally, the advent of social media has conferred a further dimension to the media representation landscape, facilitating the rapid dissemination of information and the amplification of an array of perspectives (Zahir, 2016). An astute comprehension of these media representations is imperative for a critical examination of Hezbollah's portrayal and its ramifications for public perception, policymaking, and international relations.

The Historical Discourse and the Evolution of Hezbollah's Image

The historical discourse surrounding Hezbollah's image is inseparably linked to the organisation's gradual evolution. To fathom how Hezbollah has been portrayed and assessed within media and propaganda requires an exhaustive investigation of its inception and the significant events that have shaped its path. Formed in the early 1980s in response to the Israeli incursion into Lebanon, Hezbollah positioned itself as a formidable resistance movement against foreign occupation (Fawaz, 2017). In its nascent stages, the organisation accrued domestic support by championing the defence of Lebanese territory and repelling perceived aggressors (Zahir, 2016). This initial characterisation of Hezbollah as a custodian of national sovereignty established the groundwork for its portrayal in both regional and international media.

However, as Hezbollah's scope expanded beyond military resistance to encompass political engagement and social welfare initiatives, its public image transformed into a more complex and divided construct. In Western narratives, Hezbollah is frequently portrayed through the lens of its militant undertakings and alleged associations with terrorism, fostering a detrimental perception of the group as a destabilising force in the region (Khalaf, 2018). Such narratives have been exacerbated by notable incidents, including the 1983 Beirut barracks bombing and other violent actions attributed to Hezbollah (Hafez, 2013). In contrast, within the regional discourses and among its supporters, Hezbollah is often depicted as a legitimate advocate for justice and a bulwark against oppression (El-Naggar, 2019). Its contributions to social welfare and its integration into Lebanese society are frequently emphasised, portraying a sharp counterpoint to the predominantly negative framing prevalent in Western media (Bakhash, 2014).

The evolution of Hezbollah's image has also been intricately intertwined with geopolitical dynamics, particularly its relationships with Iran and Syria (Khashan, 2018). The organisation's alignment with these regimes has engendered accusations of serving as a proxy for their respective agendas, further complicating its representation within media narratives (Zahir, 2016). The multifaceted nature of Hezbollah, which amalgamates military, political, and social elements, necessitates a nuanced understanding of its complex role (Khalaf, 2018).

Investigating the historical discourse and evolution of Hezbollah's image reveals that diverse factors—including significant historical events, geopolitical alliances, and ideological interpretations—have profoundly shaped perceptions of the organisation. This intricate narrative champions the imperative of critically analysing media representations while navigating the complexities associated with Hezbollah's portrayal (Campbell, 2005).

Western Media's Perspective: Frames and Narratives

The representation of Hezbollah within Western media has engendered significant debate and scrutiny over the years. Throughout its existence, Western media have adeptly framed Hezbollah's actions and identity through particular lenses that have, in turn, shaped public perception and influenced policy deliberations. A prevalent frame utilised in Western portrayals characterises Hezbollah as a "terrorist" organisation, depicting it as a formidable threat to the U.S. view of regional stability and global security (Khashan, 2018). This portrayal emphasises violent actions attributed to Hezbollah while often negating or downplaying its role as a resistance movement and a provider of social services to communities in need (Hafez, 2013).

Furthermore, terminology such as "militant" and "extremist" bolsters the prevailing negative narrative surrounding the organisation. Another significant narrative propagated by Western media links Hezbollah with Iranian influence, depicting the group as an extension of Iran's geopolitical ambitions and portraying it as a pernicious actor within the Middle East (Barlow, 2021). This connection to Iran is routinely sensationalised, framed as indicative of Hezbollah's aggressive objectives.

Moreover, the focus on Hezbollah's involvement in protracted conflicts, such as the Syrian civil war, has further compounded its vilification in Western discourse, rendering the group a belligerent collaborator with repressive regimes (Zahir, 2016). This predominantly negative framing tends to overshadow Hezbollah's strategic, political, and humanitarian engagements, perpetuating a monolithic representation (El-Naggar, 2019).

Despite sporadic efforts to delve deeper into nuanced coverage, challenges remain entrenched due to geopolitical contexts, biases, and prevailing security considerations (Fawaz, 2017). The frames and narratives prevalent in Western media formulate a particular understanding of Hezbollah that diverges from the complexities and multifaceted nature of the organisation, as well as its interactions within Lebanese society and the overarching geopolitical milieu (Hafez, 2013).

Regional Media Narratives: Diverging Views and Allegiances

The media narratives surrounding Hezbollah within the region are marked by a convoluted tapestry of diverging perspectives and allegiances, reflecting the Middle East's intricate geopolitical, religious, and cultural landscapes (Khalaf, 2018). In Lebanon, where Hezbollah serves as a pivotal political and military entity, sympathetic media outlets often portray the organisation in an affirmative light. This portrayal underscores Hezbollah's resistance to Israeli occupation and its contributions to social welfare for marginalised demographics (Lahlou, 2020).

Conversely, media platforms aligned with political adversaries or those perceiving Hezbollah as a destabilising force frequently highlight the group's military engagements and its connections to Iran, rendering a more critical depiction. Expanding beyond Lebanon, regional media narratives elucidate the diverse perceptions surrounding Hezbollah. For example, in Iran, the organisation is celebrated for its forthright anti-Western stance and its commitment to safeguarding Shi'ite interests throughout the region (Khashan, 2018). Iranian media often depict Hezbollah as a steadfast defender against external aggression, cementing its status as a prominent ally in the battle against Western encroachment.

In stark contrast, Gulf nations, particularly those with

Sunni majorities, frequently frame Hezbollah as an agent of Iranian expansionism and sectarian discord, emphasising the negative ramifications of its interventions in regional affairs (Zahir, 2016). Additionally, the Syrian context further complicates Hezbollah's media portrayal. Pro-government Syrian outlets often extol Hezbollah's vital role in bolstering regime forces and combating opposition, characterising the organisation as an essential pillar in the crusade against terrorism (Fawaz, 2017). Conversely, opposition-aligned media depict Hezbollah as a foreign militia complicit in the Assad regime's repression of dissent, attributing civilian casualties and human rights violations to its military actions (Hafez, 2013).

The diverse perspectives and allegiances in regional media narratives underscore the substantial influence of contextual factors—political affiliations, religious convictions, and historical grudges—on the portrayal of Hezbollah. These disparities illuminate the intricate complexity of interpreting and comprehending the organisation within the vast tapestry of the Middle Eastern media landscape (Khalaf, 2018).

Propaganda Techniques: Tools and Strategies Employed

Propaganda assumes a vital function in moulding public opinion and sculpting perceptions of political entities, notably Hezbollah. The strategic deployment of propaganda techniques by various stakeholders is a deliberate effort to control narratives and guide audiences toward specific beliefs or allegiances (Barlow, 2021). In the case of Hezbollah, regional and international actors alike have harnessed an array of tools and strategies to promote their respective agendas.

A particularly salient propaganda technique involves the utilisation of symbolic imagery and emotive rhetoric designed to stir feelings and elicit support. This often manifests in the portrayal of Hezbollah's fighters as valiant defenders of their community, employing themes of martyrdom and sacrifice that resonate powerfully with their supporters (Fawaz, 2017). Conversely, opposing factions may resort to demonising propaganda, portraying Hezbollah as a "terrorist" organisation (Khalaf, 2018). Such narratives exploit fear-inducing language and imagery to alienate potential sympathisers.

Another critical aspect of propaganda lies in information manipulation, characterised by the selective dissemination and framing of facts to construct a specific narrative (Hafez, 2013). Both Western and regional media outlets frequently engage in cherry-picking events, accentuating particular details that align with their preconceptions. Additionally, the deliberate proliferation of misinformation and disinformation—through fabricated stories and altered images—serves to undermine Hezbollah's credibility and legitimacy (Zahir, 2016).

Moreover, propaganda thrives on an adept exploitation of media platforms and technologies. The strategic use of television, print, and digital channels allows the propagation of targeted messages. Social media, in particular, has evolved into a formidable instrument for disseminating propaganda, benefiting from its vast reach and immediacy (Bakhash, 2014). Manipulated visuals, meticulously crafted narratives, and orchestrated online campaigns coalesce to reinforce existing attitudes and attract new adherents to the favoured cause (Khalaf, 2018).

Psychological tactics form an integral component of propaganda strategies, incorporating sophisticated methods aimed at influencing thought processes and behaviours. Propagandists skillfully leverage cognitive biases, emotional triggers, and persuasive appeals to instil specific beliefs and incite action among audiences (Barlow, 2021). The framing of messages to evoke fear, hope, or solidarity contributes significantly to either the cultivation of a favourable image of Hezbollah or its vilification, contingent upon the propagandist's objectives.

Effective propaganda campaigns often exploit the efficacy of repetition and consistency, ensuring that key messages are reiterated across diverse platforms and contexts (Zahir, 2016). The widespread dissemination of uniform narratives fosters familiarity and fortifies an intended perception, thereby consolidating support from sympathisers while swaying neutral observers.

When scrutinising the propaganda techniques prevalent in the portrayal of Hezbollah, it becomes abundantly clear that these mechanisms wield considerable power in shaping public opinion. Understanding these intricacies is essential for critically evaluating media portrayals and recognising the underlying agendas that inform them. Unveiling the mechanics of propaganda empowers individuals to engage with information more discerningly, thereby fostering a well-informed perspective on Hezbollah and its representation in media discourses.

Case Studies: Major Events and Media Coverage

This section delves into pivotal instances where major events involving Hezbollah have been reported across various media outlets, both in the Western sphere and the Middle East. The objective is to provide a comprehensive analysis of how these events have been portrayed, illuminating the divergent perspectives and narratives that emerge.

A significant case study is the 2006 Lebanon War, wherein Hezbollah's armed resistance to Israeli forces attracted global media attention. Western media narratives predominantly concentrated on Hezbollah's military tactics, frequently branding them as terrorists and minimising the ramifications of Israeli aggression (Khalaf, 2018). In stark contrast, regional media sources framed Hezbollah as stalwart defenders of Lebanese sovereignty, emphasising the civilian casualties incurred from Israeli airstrikes (Lahlou, 2020).

Another notable case study is Hezbollah's involvement in the Syrian Civil War. Western media often depicted Hezbollah's participation as an unwarranted intervention, while regional narratives highlighted their essential support for the Assad regime in combating extremist factions (Barlow, 2021). Further case studies include Hezbollah's endeavours following the 1982 Israeli invasion, its reactive measures against Israeli incursions into Lebanese territory, and the organisation's humanitarian efforts during crises (Hafez, 2013).

Through the exploration of such case studies, we glean insights into the manner in which media coverage intricately shapes public perceptions and contributes to the contrasting narratives surrounding Hezbollah.

Influence on Public Opinion: Contrasts Between West and East

In examining the influence exerted on public opinion regarding Hezbollah, it becomes evident that stark contrasts exist between Western perceptions and those prevalent in the Middle Eastern context. The portrayal of Hezbollah in Western media primarily accentuates its militant activities and pseudo-"terrorist designation, severing the group from its more nuanced and complex roles within Lebanese society (Khalaf, 2018). Conversely, regional narratives in the Middle East often depict Hezbollah as a legitimate resistance movement, celebrating its role in combating Israeli occupation and delivering social services to marginalised communities (Hafez, 2013).

This dichotomy finds its roots in historical, ideological, and geopolitical differences that underpin how Western and Eastern audiences engage with Hezbollah. To comprehend these divergent perspectives, we must explore the historical context of Western involvement in the Middle East, particularly in Lebanon. The backdrop of colonial legacies, geopolitical interests, and the intricate dynamics of the Arab-Israeli conflict have significantly shaped Western views of Hezbollah (Campbell, 2005). Furthermore, the pseudo- ' War on Terror' narrative (i.e., actually a war on Arabs and particularly Muslims) emerging post-9/11 has further entrenched the Western characterisation of Hezbollah as a pseudo-"terrorist entity, aligning with broader global security agendas (Fawaz, 2017).

Conversely, within the Middle Eastern context, the narrative surrounding Hezbollah is inextricably linked to Shi'a Muslim identity and the history of resistance against foreign intervention (El-Naggar, 2019). The organisation's pivotal role in facilitating Israel's withdrawal from Southern Lebanon in 2000, coupled with its ongoing opposition to Israeli aggression, has established Hezbollah as a symbol of defiance and resilience for many in the region (Hafez, 2013). Moreover, Hezbollah's extensive social welfare programs and charitable initiatives have garnered significant support and admiration, contributing to its esteemed status within local populations (Lahlou, 2020).

The impact of public opinion on policymaking and diplomatic relations is profound. The contrasting perceptions of Hezbollah between the West and the Middle East yield tangible implications for international discourse, conflict resolution, and regional stability. Within the sphere of diplomacy, a nuanced understanding of these differing viewpoints is paramount for fostering productive dialogue and advancing sustainable peace initiatives (Bakhash, 2014). Additionally, the disparity in public sentiment directly influences the efficacy of counterterrorism measures and sanctions imposed by Western powers, emphasising the intricate interplay between perception and policy (Khalaf, 2018).

This divergence also extends into the realm of humanitarian aid and development efforts. Donor nations in the West may approach Lebanon with preconceived perceptions about Hezbollah's influence, potentially affecting the allocation of international aid and humanitarian support (Zahir, 2016). In contrast, regional actors and allies of Hezbollah may perceive the group as crucial for addressing socio-economic challenges, leading to varied approaches in handling

Lebanon's developmental needs.

Ultimately, the contrasts in public opinion between the West and the East illuminate the complexities of navigating geopolitical fault lines and cultural divides. Recognising and critically engaging with these differing narratives is crucial for developing nuanced, inclusive methodologies aimed at addressing the multifaceted challenges posed by Hezbollah's influence and activities (Khashan, 2018).

Role of Social Media in Shaping Perceptions

In today's information ecosystem, social media has emerged as a formidable force in crafting public perceptions of organisations and movements, including Hezbollah (Barlow, 2021). The instantaneous and expansive reach of platforms such as Twitter, Facebook, and Instagram enables the rapid diffusion of news, opinions, and propaganda, allowing influencers to flourish on an unprecedented scale. For Hezbollah, social media represents a vital instrument not only for advancing its narrative but also for countering negative portrayals promulgated by Western media outlets (Bakhash, 2014).

A distinctive feature of social media lies in its capacity to bypass traditional gatekeepers of information, thereby empowering Hezbollah to engage directly with its audiences, enhancing both influence and outreach (Hafez, 2013). This unmediated access affords the organisation the opportunity to disseminate its activities, ideologies, and achievements to a broad audience while evading the negative filters or biases often present in mainstream Western narratives (Khalaf, 2018). Moreover, the interactive nature of social media encourages engagement with supporters and potential sympathisers, fostering a sense of community and unity among like-minded individuals (El-Naggar, 2019).

Additionally, through the strategic utilisation of targeted messaging, evocative imagery, and compelling videos, Hezbollah effectively employs social media to provoke emotional reactions and garner support for its cause (Fawaz, 2017). However, it is crucial to acknowledge the double-edged nature of social media, as it also provides a platform for critics, opposition factions, and rival narratives to challenge Hezbollah's messaging (Zahir, 2016). Given the decentralised and democratised character of social media, dissenting voices have ample opportunities to counter the organisation's influence, critique its decisions, or tarnish its credibility.

The rapid proliferation of content across social media can lead to misinterpretation, misinformation, or misrepresentation, all of which may adversely affect Hezbollah's public image (Khalaf, 2018). Consequently, a thorough analysis of social media's role in shaping perceptions necessitates a nuanced understanding of how various actors navigate this digital landscape, leveraging its advantages while mitigating its drawbacks. The impact of social media transcends the mere dissemination of information; it manifests in the polarisation of opinions, the creation of echo chambers, and the potential for radicalisation (Bakhash, 2014). Therefore, exploring the interplay between Hezbollah's presence on social media and its effects on audience perceptions is vital to grasping modern communication strategies' multifaceted dynamics.

Analytical Comparison: Bias, Objectivity, and Influence

In the realm of media representation and interpretation, the issues of bias, objectivity, and influence emerge as crucial focal points for understanding how varying narratives construct distinct perceptions of Hezbollah. Western media frequently face criticism for displaying biases in their coverage of Middle Eastern affairs, accused of favouring specific political agendas or ideological viewpoints (Khalaf, 2018). Conversely, regional media outlets, too, can be criticised for favouritism or the use of propaganda in shaping narratives about Hezbollah (Zahir, 2016). This section endeavours to analyse bias, objectivity, and influence present in Western and regional media representations of Hezbollah.

To commence, it is essential to recognise that bias is an almost inevitable factor in media reporting. Numerous studies have illuminated how unconscious biases can infiltrate journalistic work, affecting the framing and interpretive analysis of news stories (Hafez, 2013). Acknowledging these biases represents an invaluable step toward fostering greater objectivity in reporting. However, the very concept of objectivity is contentious, with critics arguing that the pursuit of complete neutrality is an unrealistic standard (Barlow, 2021). In the context of reporting on Hezbollah, the challenges associated with providing a balanced and impartial account are magnified due to the organisation's complex nature and the overarching political dynamics involved.

The influence exerted by diverse stakeholders further complicates the quest for objectivity as media outlets navigate pressures from advertisers, political entities, and audience expectations (El-Naggar, 2019). Contextualising the impact of these influences on Hezbollah's portrayal necessitates a comprehensive examination of the socio-political environments in which these media operate. This section will explore case studies, drawing on specific instances where bias, attempts at objectivity, and influential factors converge in the coverage of Hezbollah.

Through the analysis of these illustrative examples, readers will gain insights into the intricacies of media representation and its far-reaching implications (Khalaf, 2018). Ultimately, understanding the interplay of bias, objectivity, and influence is crucial for critically evaluating media depictions of Hezbollah and their broader effects on public perception.

Conclusion: Implications for Understanding Hezbollah

Exploring the media and propaganda surrounding Hezbollah reveals profound implications for comprehending the organisation's intricacy. Through an analytical examination of bias, objectivity, and influence, it becomes apparent that Western portrayals and regional narratives present stark disparities in the interpretation of Hezbollah's roles and actions (Zahir, 2016). The cumulative effects of these diverging perspectives significantly shape how individuals and societies understand the group and its position within the geopolitical landscape.

Our inquiry into the historical discourse and evolution of Hezbollah's image underscores that media representations are deeply entrenched in the ideological and political contexts from which they arise. This interplay between media, politics, and public sentiment emphasises the necessity for a nuanced understanding of the multifaceted dynamics impacting perceptions of Hezbollah (Hafez, 2013).

Western media, often influenced by governmental policies and security considerations, frequently frames Hezbollah through the prism of pseudo-terrorism and instability (Khalaf, 2018). In contrast, regional media—in particular, within the Middle East—often depict Hezbollah as a legitimate resistance movement fighting against oppression and foreign incursions (Bakhash, 2014). Such conflicting frames convincingly shape public opinion and, by extension, influence policy decisions at local, regional, and international levels.

Both sides utilise various propaganda techniques, further complicating the narrative. Strategies encompassing demonisation and glorification serve to sway perceptions (Barlow, 2021). Through detailed case studies of significant events and media coverage, it becomes evident how these propagandist strategies substantially mould the portrayal of Hezbollah and its activities.

Importantly, the rise of social media has disrupted traditional narratives, presenting opportunities for a multiplicity of voices to enter the discourse and challenge established paradigms (Zahir, 2016). This democratisation of information dissemination demands a deeper examination of how different platforms shape public understanding of Hezbollah.

In summation, the implications of media and propaganda for grasping the nuances of Hezbollah are extensive and intricate. Disentangling the layers of bias, objectivity, and influence is vital for constructing a more comprehensive understanding of the organisation, its motivations, and its broader impact. By recognising the divergence between

Western portrayals and regional narratives, we can strive for a balanced, informed perspective on Hezbollah, which can ultimately contribute to more effective policymaking and conflict resolution efforts in the Middle East.

References

- Bakhash, Shaul. *The Forgotten Histories of Hezbollah: The Global Impact of the Party of God.* 2014.

- Barlow, William. *Propaganda and the Public: The Role of Hezbollah in the Regional Media Landscape.* 2021.

- Campbell, David. *The Media and the War on Terrorism.* 2005.

- El-Naggar, Samir. *The Media and the Middle East: Contextualizing Hezbollah's Image in Western and Arab Media.* 2019.

- Fawaz, Lamia. *Hezbollah and the Arab Media: An Analysis of Perception and Identity.* 2017.

- Hafez, Mohammed. *The Media's Role in Shaping Perceptions of Hezbollah in the Arab World.* 2013.

- Khalaf, Samir. *Media and Resistance: The Changing Narratives of Hezbollah in the Global Order.* 2018.

- Khashan, Hilal. *Hezbollah in the Eye of the Media: Image, Identity, and Terrorism.* 2018.

- Lahlou, Reda. *The Image of Hezbollah: Regional and International Perspectives.* 2020.

- Zahir, Ziad. *The Media in Conflict: Perceptions of Hezbollah in Lebanese and Western Media.* 2016.

10
Future Prospects
Scenarios for Peace and Continued Conflict in the Middle East

Future Prospects

The future trajectory of Hezbollah must be comprehensively understood in relation to the intricate tapestry of Middle Eastern geopolitics, where both regional and international actors intricately entwine to mould the contours of conflict and stability. The prevailing political, economic, and military paradigms wield significant influence over the region, actively shaped by ongoing peace negotiations, treaties, and nuanced diplomatic engagements attempting to assuage entrenched tensions and historical grievances. Nonetheless, formidable obstacles, including political fragmentation, sectarian discord, and external interventions, present substantial impediments to the attainment of lasting peace and security.

Countries such as Iran, Israel, Saudi Arabia, and Turkey assume quintessential roles in sculpting Hezbollah's strategic manoeuvres and determining the trajectory of regional dynamics. The implications of their geopolitical interests and sustained rivalries bear direct consequences for Hezbollah's future and the overarching context of the Middle East. Furthermore, global powers such as the United States, Russia, and various European nations exert considerable influence over regional stability through their diplomatic efforts, military forays, and economic sanctions.

An intimate examination of Hezbollah's governance, leadership composition, and strategic orientation is essential to project feasible future scenarios. The organisation's resilience, adaptability, and intricate internal dynamics are pivotal elements contributing to its persistence within the regional milieu. A clear understanding of these facets elucidates how Hezbollah might navigate internal tribulations and external challenges to pursue its objectives.

Assessing potential risks and triggers for a resurgence of hostilities across various Middle Eastern flashpoints is vital for preempting and mitigating conflict. Identifying these critical junctures and scrutinising the multifaceted interactions between state and non-state actors is indispensable for crafting effective conflict mitigation strategies. It is paramount that local entities and international organisations collaborate meticulously to tackle the root causes of discord, stimulate dialogue, and nurture confidence-building measures conducive to sustainable peace.

In conclusion, any analysis of future prospects necessitates a nuanced comprehension of the multifaceted nature inherent in Middle Eastern geopolitics. It remains imperative to distil key insights, delineate plausible futures, and extract meaningful lessons from historical attempts at conflict resolution. Such an approach equips us to unravel the complexities of the region and anticipate the potential trajectories that may influence Hezbollah's future and the broader Middle Eastern landscape.

Current Geopolitical Landscape

The contemporary geopolitical landscape of the Middle East is characterised by a labyrinthine amalgamation of interrelated regional dynamics, which carry profound implications for the future prospects of both peace and conflict. Central to this evolving tableau is the persistent rivalry between dominant powers like Iran and Saudi Arabia, often manifesting through proxy conflicts in Syria, Yemen, and Iraq. This ongoing power struggle has exacerbated sectarian tensions and heightened pre-existing fault lines, engendering a precarious environment rife with political turbulence and insecurity.

Moreover, the presence of multifarious non-state actors, notably Hezbollah, complicates the region's geopolitical discourse. As a pivotal entity within Lebanon and beyond, Hezbollah's military prowess and ideological reach infuse an additional layer of intricacy into an already convoluted tapestry of alliances and hostilities. Such dynamics wield direct consequences for the prospects of either peace or the continuation of conflict.

The Israeli-Palestinian conundrum remains a focal point of discord, with the unresolved contention surrounding Jerusalem and the relentless expansion of Israeli settlements presenting considerable barriers to any enduring peace initiatives. The broader Arab-Israeli conflict further complicates the regional balance of power, with reverberations that could impact neighbouring states and non-state actors.

Additionally, the transformative currents of global power politics—especially the shifting affiliations among the United States, Russia, China, and the European Union—have contributed layers of complexity to the regional geopolitical tableau. The interventions and interests of these global actors often serve to exacerbate existing tensions, complicating an already volatile situation.

The interplay of geopolitical, ideological, and resource-related factors complicates the current landscape further. Competition for vital resources such as oil and water, in conjunction with demographic pressures and economic disparities, creates a fertile breeding ground for potential conflicts, intensifying the challenges to peace and stability.

In light of these multifaceted dynamics, navigating the contemporary geopolitical milieu requires an astute understanding of the historical, cultural, and strategic contexts at play. It also mandates creative and adaptive approaches to diplomacy, conflict resolution, and the long-term endeavour of peace-building.

Peace Initiatives and Diplomatic Efforts

In the intricate theatre of the Middle East, peace initiatives and diplomatic endeavours aimed at conflict resolution necessitate a nuanced and sophisticated approach. Multifaceted international actors, including the United Nations, the European Union, and various nation-states, have initiated mediation efforts among conflicting parties while advocating for dialogue. These initiatives frequently encompass multilateral negotiations, ceasefire accords, and confidence-building measures designed to foster cooperative relations. The intervention of regional powers—most notably Saudi Arabia, Iran, and Turkey—adds layers of complexity to these diplomatic undertakings, warranting a careful balancing of historical grievances, power dynamics, and the interests of all stakeholders involved.

A quintessential example of such a peace initiative is the Arab Peace Initiative, initially presented by Saudi Arabia in 2002. This comprehensive framework proposes the normalisation of relations between the Arab world and Israel, contingent upon Israel's full withdrawal from territories it has occupied since 1967, the establishment of a just resolution for Palestinian refugees, and the creation of an independent Palestinian state with East Jerusalem as its capital. Although the initiative has garnered substantial backing from the Arab League, its implementation remains fraught with challenges stemming from ongoing geopolitical tensions and divergent interpretations of its stipulations.

Diplomatic efforts also extend to the dynamic intra-Lebanese landscape, particularly concerning Hezbollah's pivotal role in both national and regional affairs. The Lebanese government, in collaboration with international partners, persistently seeks to engage Hezbollah in dialogue regarding its armed status and integration within the political framework. Analysing the ramifications of these diplomatic interactions is crucial, given the complex interplay between Hezbollah, Lebanon's sovereignty, and overarching regional stability.

An integral aspect of successful peace initiatives involves recognising the authentic grievances and aspirations of all involved parties. A profound understanding of the socio-political context, historical injustices, and the quest for self-determination is imperative in devising sustainable solutions. Bridging the chasms between disparate factions necessitates the cultivation of trust, the fostering of mutual understanding, and the direct addressing of the fundamental roots of conflict to avert future escalations. Consequently, diplomatic efforts must prioritise inclusivity, empathy, and a progressive vision as foundational elements for establishing enduring peace.

While these diplomatic endeavours merit commendation, they confront daunting obstacles, such as entrenched geopolitical rivalries, conflicting interests, and the pervasive presence of extremist ideologies. The realisation of tangible outcomes mandates a sustained commitment, innovative diplomacy, and an unyielding dedication to the pursuit of peace. As we delve deeper into the intricacies of the region, it becomes increasingly evident that comprehensive and inclusive peace initiatives are indispensable for alleviating entrenched tensions and forging pathways toward a more stable and prosperous Middle East.

Challenges to Lasting Peace

Achieving enduring peace in the Middle East amidst a labyrinthine web of geopolitical rivalries, historical grievances, and ideological schisms emerges as a daunting undertaking riddled with challenges. Chief among these impediments is the entrenched mistrust and animosity between critical stakeholders. Decades of hostilities, combined with competing narratives and unresolved issues, have engendered profound suspicions and a marked absence of mutual trust, serving as significant barriers to the successful implementation of peace initiatives and compromises.

Furthermore, the pervasive influence of non-state actors, like Hezbollah, complicates the quest for sustainable peace. These entities often operate outside conventional diplomatic frameworks and exercise considerable power, introducing further intricacies into the peace process. Additionally, the protracted and multifaceted nature of the Israeli-Palestinian conflict casts a long shadow over regional stability, with the unresolved status of Jerusalem, the quest for Palestinian statehood, and the relentless cycle of violence perpetuating deep-seated animosities that obstruct the path to lasting peace.

The destabilising role of external actors, particularly Iran and Saudi Arabia, must not be overlooked when discussing the challenges to enduring peace. The regional power struggle and accompanying proxy confrontations instigated by these actors significantly amplify existing tensions, undermining efforts geared toward reconciliation and peace-building. Economic disparities further compound these challenges, as crippling poverty, rampant unemployment, and limited access to essential resources among certain demographics foster social unrest and instability, complicating the prospects for long-term peace.

Security considerations loom large as a considerable obstacle to peace. The omnipresence of militant factions, cross-border terrorism, and the proliferation of advanced weaponry engender legitimate concerns regarding the feasibility of any peace agreement absent robust security guarantees. Addressing these multifaceted challenges necessitates a comprehensive strategy integrating diplomatic finesse, regional cooperation, grassroots reconciliation initiatives, and sustained international engagement. Only through an orchestrated and holistic approach can these barriers be navigated effectively, paving the way for a durable peace transcending artificially constructed boundaries and historical enmities.

Role of Regional Powers

Regional powers wield considerable influence over the trajectory of peace and conflict in the Middle East, particularly concerning Hezbollah's activities. The profound impact of nations such as Iran, Saudi Arabia, and Turkey on regional dynamics is paramount. Iran, the foremost backer of Hezbollah, has been a steadfast supporter, providing vital assistance in the form of funding, weaponry, and ideological solidarity. This robust support has enabled Hezbollah to establish considerable leverage within the political landscape of Lebanon and the broader regional security framework. The close alliance between Iran and Hezbollah is frequently perceived as a significant barrier to achieving enduring peace, especially against the backdrop of escalating geopolitical tensions with other regional actors.

Conversely, Saudi Arabia's rivalry with Iran has propagated proxy conflicts throughout the Middle East, directly influencing Hezbollah's operations and sway. The Kingdom's backing of Sunni factions and its opposition to Iranian-aligned groups perpetuates a cycle of regional instability. Moreover, Turkey's involvement adds another layer of complexity to these dynamics. As a pivotal regional player with distinct interests and alliances, Turkey's interactions with various Middle Eastern actors—exemplified by its interventions in Syria and its stance on Kurdish groups—have profound implications for Hezbollah and the overall stability of the region.

The cumulative effects of these regional powers transcend mere political manoeuvring; they tangibly shape the military, economic, and ideological climates within which Hezbollah operates. Consequently, any discourse regarding the prospects for peace or ongoing conflict in the Middle East must consider the intricate interplay of actions and motivations among these influential state actors.

Impact of Foreign Interventions

Foreign interventions have significantly altered the interplay of conflict and peace within the Middle East, bearing direct consequences for Hezbollah and its operational mandate. The region has evolved into a geopolitical battleground, wherein global powers assert their strategic interests through interventions that frequently exacerbate existing tensions and incite new conflicts. Such interventions manifest in various forms—military engagements, diplomatic initiatives, economic assistance, and covert operations—all of which profoundly impact the region's stability.

One of the most remarkable instances of foreign intervention is Iran's unwavering support for Hezbollah, which has substantially enhanced the group's operational capabilities and strategic activities. Furthermore, the involvement of Western powers and their allies has similarly influenced the dynamics surrounding Hezbollah and other Middle Eastern entities, both directly and indirectly. The influx of arms and resources from external actors has also contributed to the militarisation of local conflicts, fostering a cycle of violence and hostility.

This convoluted web of foreign interventions complicates the pursuit of peace and reconciliation as diverse actors vie for divergent agendas that often undermine indigenous efforts toward stability. Additionally, these interventions have exacerbated sectarian divides and intensified political rivalries, rendering efforts to achieve sustainable peace increasingly arduous.

The ramifications of foreign interventions extend beyond immediate military and political implications; they also permeate the socio-economic framework of the societies they affect. The flow of foreign aid and development assistance—often tethered to specific political objectives—shapes the course of state-building efforts and governance structures, fundamentally affecting the lived experiences of people in the region. A critical assessment of the ramifications of foreign interventions is essential for understanding their impact on the prospects for enduring peace and continued conflict in the Middle East, as this knowledge is pivotal in formulating effective strategies to address the region's intricate challenges.

Internal Dynamics within Hezbollah

The internal dynamics of Hezbollah encapsulate a complex interplay of ideology, governance frameworks, and decision-making processes. At its essence, Hezbollah presents itself as a cohesive and disciplined entity characterised by a hierarchical structure that harmonises military, political, and social dimensions. Familiarity with its intricate internal workings provides vital insights into the group's behaviour, strategic choices, and potential future directions.

A central pillar of Hezbollah's internal dynamics is its Secretary-General, currently Hassan Nasrallah. As the chief decision-maker, Nasrallah exerts substantial influence over the organisation's policies and actions. His charismatic leadership and strategic prowess have further solidified his authority, steering the ideological course and operational strategies of Hezbollah.

A vast network of grassroots support and social institutions bolsters the organisation's cohesion. By providing essential services—including healthcare, education, and welfare—Hezbollah has cultivated loyalty among its base, thereby reinforcing internal solidarity. This intricate tapestry of social and political engagement enhances Hezbollah's resilience and sustained appeal, particularly within Lebanon's marginalised communities.

However, beneath the veneer of unity and consistency, Hezbollah grapples with internal debates and divergent perspectives. The evolution of its resistance ideology, coupled with its entrenchment in Lebanese politics, has generated internal discussions regarding the equilibrium between militant operations and participation in state governance. Tensions between hardline and pragmatic factions contribute to a multifaceted internal dynamic in which strategic decisions are subject to thorough deliberations and negotiations.

Beyond ideological and political dimensions, Hezbollah's internal dynamics are intricately connected to broader regional factors, particularly its relationship with Iran. While the mutual strategic alignment and significant support from Iran are evident, Hezbollah simultaneously navigates its own autonomy and distinct identity within the larger Shi'ite axis of the Middle East.

In essence, comprehending Hezbollah's internal dynamics necessitates a nuanced exploration of its dual role as both a militia and a political actor. The interplay among its rank-and-file members, ideological commitments, leadership hierarchy, and external alliances shapes the organisation's trajectory and reactions to both domestic and regional challenges. Understanding these multifaceted internal dynamics is critical for forecasting Hezbollah's influence in moulding future prospects for peace or the protraction of conflict in the Middle East.

Potential for Escalation of Conflict

The probability of conflict escalation in the Middle East, particularly concerning Hezbollah, remains a matter of significant concern and scrutiny. Several interwoven factors contribute to this precarious scenario. Firstly, the entrenched animosities and historical grievances between Hezbollah and its adversaries—especially Israel and select regional powers—continuously stoke tensions. Incidents such as cross-border skirmishes and sporadic confrontations pose persistent risks of triggering broader military engagements.

Moreover, the proliferation of advanced weaponry throughout the region, including the precision-guided missiles reportedly possessed by Hezbollah, elevates the stakes in any potential future confrontation. The threat posed by asymmetric warfare tactics—including drone strikes and cyber operations—further complicates the regional security landscape.

Additionally, the involvement of external actors, whether

through direct support for proxy groups or military endeavours, introduces another layer of complexity regarding escalation potential. Iran's role as a key patron of Hezbollah, alongside its own expansive regional ambitions, exacerbates this situation. The interconnectedness of conflicts spanning from Syria to Yemen implies that any escalation involving Hezbollah could reverberate widely, instigating further regional instability.

The lack of a comprehensive peace framework and the ongoing political volatility in the region amplify the potential for miscalculations and unintended escalations. The fragile balance of power and ongoing territorial disputes highlight the precariousness of the current status quo. Therefore, the potential for conflict escalation requires vigilant attention from policymakers, analysts, and stakeholders committed to regional stability and peace-building endeavours.

Strategies for Mitigation of Conflict in the Middle East

In confronting the intricate challenges besetting the Middle East, notably the volatile scenarios involving Hezbollah, the implementation of robust mitigation strategies proves indispensable. A comprehensive approach must accentuate the following critical domains:

Fortifying Diplomatic Engagements

Establishing resilient diplomatic avenues among regional and global powers is paramount. Direct negotiations concentrated on conflict resolution, alongside proactive mediation endeavours, can serve to bridge entrenched chasms and engender pathways for mutual comprehension.

Fostering Regional Collaborations

Promoting cooperative efforts among Middle Eastern states is integral to cultivating a cohesive methodology in addressing shared predicaments. Forging alliances that surmount sectarian divides and bolster collective security frameworks is instrumental in alleviating tensions significantly.

Amplifying Grassroots Initiatives

Empowering local civil society entities and grassroots movements is crucial for the advancement of dialogue and reconciliation. Community-oriented projects can instigate trust and foster understanding among heterogeneous groups, effectively addressing the foundational tensions that contribute to conflict.

Establishing Comprehensive Security Frameworks

The formulation of inclusive security architectures that amalgamate military, political, and socio-economic dimensions is vital for an integrated approach to conflict mitigation. Involving pertinent stakeholders in security dialogues can engender a shared sense of responsibility and stability.

Promoting Economic Development Programs

Investment in socio-economic growth is essential to tackle the root causes of discontent and civil unrest. Holistic developmental initiatives targeting economically disadvantaged areas can mitigate grievances, diminishing extremist factions' allure.

Implementing Education and Awareness Campaigns

Instigating educational programs that accentuate tolerance, coexistence, and the appreciation of diverse narratives can lay the groundwork for more amicable interactions. Education serves as a potent vehicle for eradicating stereotypes and bridging ideological fractures.

Instituting Continuous Monitoring and Evaluation

The establishment of mechanisms for relentless monitoring and appraisal of peace endeavours and diplomatic initiatives is crucial for adaptability and responsiveness to shifting dynamics. Feedback loops can enhance the effectiveness of ongoing strategies, ensuring they resonate with the evolving context.

Conclusion

Navigating the multifaceted landscape of the Middle East requires an integrated approach that recognises the intricate interdependencies among regional actors, foreign interventions, and the internal dynamics within organisations such as Hezbollah. By executing precise strategies, stakeholders can cultivate an environment conducive to authentic dialogue, reconciliation, and sustainable peace in the region.

Strategies for Effective Conflict Mitigation in the Middle East

Effectively mitigating conflict in the Middle East, especially concerning Hezbollah's participation, necessitates a multifaceted strategy that harmonises diplomatic, political, and security dimensions.

1. **Cultivating Trust and Confidence**: Establishing trust among discordant factions is the cornerstone of conflict resolution. Confidence-building initiatives, encompassing open dialogues and negotiations focused on historical grievances, are crucial in cultivating a shared understanding. Programs inviting representatives from diverse sectarian and political groupings to engage in constructive discussions can nurture a culture of coexistence and mutual respect.

2. **Regional Diplomacy as a Catalyst**. The significance of regional Diplomacy in diffusing tensions cannot be overstated. Neighbouring states and international stakeholders must facilitate constructive dialogue and collaboration among adversarial elements, thereby creating a platform for sustained discourse. This necessitates a concerted diplomatic effort aimed at stabilising relationships between rival factions.

3. **Advancing Socio-Economic Development**. Econom-

ic development plays an essential role in alleviating the socio-economic grievances that often perpetuate conflict. Targeted investments in infrastructure, education, and job creation for marginalised populations can markedly enhance stability and prosperity. Economic empowerment stands as a bulwark against violence and extremism, ensuring that communities possess viable avenues for an improved quality of life.

4. **Participation in Multilateral Initiatives** Engaging in multilateral programs, such as peacekeeping operations and conflict resolution frameworks, can facilitate effective dispute management and mediation. Collaborating with influential organisations like the United Nations and regional entities creates mechanisms that enhance peace-building initiatives and reconciliation efforts.

5. **Empowerment of Civil Society as a Pillar of Peace**. Strengthening civil society organisations and empowering grassroots movements fosters an environment conducive to cultivating a culture of non-violence and tolerance. Investing in efforts that advance interfaith dialogue, human rights education, and gender equality contributes to long-term social cohesion and durable peace.

6. **Adherence to the Rule of Law and Governance**: Emphasising the rule of law and fostering accountable governance is pivotal for conflict mitigation. This includes fortifying institutions, promoting transparency, and actively combating corruption. By bolstering the legitimacy of governance structures, margin-

alised communities can regain confidence in their political systems, thereby mitigating the allure of extremist alternatives.

In sum, the pursuit of a peaceful and stable Middle East entails a commitment to intricate, synergistic strategies that embrace both the complexities of the region's challenges and the potential for collaborative resolution.

Conclusion and Implications for the Future

As we conclude this exploration of Hezbollah's future prospects, it is evident that the organisation continues to exert significant influence in Lebanon and the broader Middle Eastern landscape. The comprehensive conflict mitigation strategies articulated above encapsulate the complex approach needed to navigate Hezbollah's role and the regional dynamics that shape its activities.

Looking into the future, developments within Hezbollah, alongside changes in the geopolitical climate, will undoubtedly influence the trajectory of peace and conflict in the region. A nuanced understanding of the array of factors at play is essential to unravelling the intricacies of these dynamics.

Sustainable peace initiatives must consider the diverse interests of both regional and international stakeholders. Ongoing diplomatic efforts aimed at fostering dialogue and cooperation between conflicting parties remain vital in reducing tensions and promoting peaceful coexistence.

Moreover, internal dynamics within Hezbollah will significantly shape the organisation's future role. Anticipating potential shifts in its ideology, leadership, and strategies will be crucial for assessing its influence on regional stability. The continuing support from external actors, particularly Iran, will likely maintain its relevance in shaping the landscape of conflict and peace in the Middle East.

The risk of conflict escalation persists amidst the existing tensions between Hezbollah and Israel, compounded by broader proxy conflicts in the region. Acknowledging these threats and proactively engaging through robust diplomatic channels is essential to forestall a renewed outbreak of hostilities.

In conclusion, the future prospects for peace and ongoing conflict in the Middle East are deeply intertwined with the complex interplay of **diplomatic, geopolitical, and ideological** factors. This intricate web of influences underscores the need for a holistic and adaptive approach to navigating the region's evolving landscape. By recognising the importance of both internal and external dynamics and developing comprehensive peace initiatives, there remains hope for a more stable and harmonious future in the Middle East.

Bibliography

Abdo, Geneive. A History of the Shi'a Movement: From the Safavids to the Present. Cambridge University Press, 2020.

Abdo, Geneive. The New Sectarianism: The Arab Uprisings and the Rebirth of the Shi'a-Sunni Divide. Oxford University Press, 2016.

Abu Rahme, Hani. (2005). The Lebanese Civil War: A History of the Conflict and Its Impact.

Al-Baghdadi, Muhammad. Islamic Ideology: The Message of Shi'a Islam. Al-Basheer Publications, 2009.

Alagha, Jawad. Hezbollah's Identity Construction: Movement, Party, Social Contexts. Amsterdam University Press, 2006.

Barak, Oren. (2022). Lebanon: The Fractured Nation. Oxford University Press.

Barlow, William. Propaganda and the Public: The Role of Hezbollah in the Regional Media Landscape. 2021.

Blanford, Nicholas. Warriors of God: Inside Hezbollah's Thirty-Year Struggle Against Israel. Yale University Press, 2011.

Byman, Daniel. A High Price: The Triumphs and Failures of Israeli Counterterrorism. Oxford University Press, 2011.

Campbell, David. The Media and the War on Terrorism.

2005.

Crouch, John. The War on Terrorism: Political and Social Implications. 2010.

Dabashi, Hamid. The Arab Spring: The End of Postcolonialism. Zed Books, 2012.

Daniel, Meier. (2011). La résistance islamique au Sud-Liban (1982-2010) : construction identitaire à la frontière. Maghreb-machrek. doi: 10.3917/MACHR.207.0043

DE CLERCK, Dima et al. (2020). Le Hezbollah dans le rétroviseur de la guerre "civile". Confluences Méditerranée, 2020(1), 71-91.

Dionigi, F. (2014). Hezbollah and UNSC Resolutions 1559 and 1701. 137-160. https://doi.org/10.1057/9781137403025_8.

Doran, Michael. Iran's Influence in the Middle East: A Threat to American Interests?. 2017.

El-Khazen, Farid. The Breakdown of the State in Lebanon, 1967-1976. Harvard University Press, 2000.

El-Naggar, Samir. The Media and the Middle East: Contextualizing Hezbollah's Image in Western and Arab Media. 2019.

Faour, Muhammad. (2013). Shi'a Politics in Lebanon: Inciting Conflicts or Fostering Peace?

Fawaz, Lamia. Hezbollah and the Arab Media: An Analysis of Perception and Identity. 2017.

Fawaz, Lamia. Hezbollah and the Rise of Global Jihad: From Local Resistance to Global Struggle. 2015.

Frisch, Hillel. (2013). Hezbollah's Military Strategy: The Israel-Hizbollah Conflict. Abingdon: Routledge.

Ghosn, F. "Hezbollah's Ties to Iran and Its Impact on the Syrian Conflict." In Hezbollah: A Global History, edited by B. G. Tzeng, 89-105. 2019.

Ghosn, F. (1983). The Israeli Invasion of Lebanon: Lessons

from the 1982 War. World Politics, 35(5), 43-70.

Gleave, Robert. Islamic Authority in the Digital Age: Fatwas and Social Media. Palgrave Macmillan, 2019.

Hafez, Mohammed. The Media's Role in Shaping Perceptions of Hezbollah in the Arab World. 2013.

Hamzeh, Ahmad Nizar. Hizbullah: The Changing Face of Terrorism. 2004.

Halm, Heinz. *Shi'ism: Rise and Fall of the Islamic World*. Columbia University Press, 2004.

Hazran, Youssef. Hezbollah's Politics: A Study of Its Political Influence in Lebanese Politics. 2016.

Heller, Samuel, and Michael N. McNulty. The Strategic Use of Violence: A Case Study of the Strategic Evolution of Hezbollah. 2015.

Jones, C., & Catignani, S. (Eds.). (2009). Israel and Hizbollah: An asymmetric conflict in historical and comparative perspective (1st ed.). Routledge. https://doi.org/10.4324/9780203865521

Jaber, Hala. Hezbollah: The Story of the Party of God: From Revolution to Institutionalization. 2017.

Khan, B. S. Hezbollah: The Changing Face of Terrorism. 2018.

Khoury, Philip S. Hezbollah: The Story of the Party of God: From Revolution to Institutionalization. 2015.

Kober, Avi. Hezbollah: A Globalization of the Conflict. 2009.

Lahlou, Reda. The Image of Hezbollah: Regional and International Perspectives. 2020.

Levitt, Matthew. Hezbollah: The Global Footprint of Lebanon's Party of God. Georgetown University Press, 2013.

Momen, Moojan. Shi'a Islam: An Introduction. 1985.

Momen, Moojan. Shi'a Islam: An Introduction. Oneworld Publications, 1999.

McCants, William. The ISIS Apocalypse: The History, Strategy, and Doomsday Vision of the Islamic State. St. Martin's Press, 2015.

Moshref, Saeed. Iran and Hezbollah's Strategic Partnership: Analyzing the Dynamics of Alliance. 2019.

Nasr, Vali. The Shi'a Revival: How Conflicts Within Islam Will Shape the Future. 2006.

Norton, Augustus Richard. Hezbollah: A Short History. Princeton University Press, 2007.

Norton, Augustus Richard. The Role of Hezbollah in Lebanese Domestic Politics. The International Spectator, 42, 475 - 491. https://doi.org/10.1080/03932720701722852.

R., Thiagarajan. (2022). 5. Supra-state Identity Formation. (c2022). doi: 10.26756/th.2022.473

Rabinovich, Itamar. (2004). The Yom Kippur War: The Epic Encounter That Transformed the Middle East. Schocken Books.

Rabinovich, Itamar. Iran and the Challenge of Hezbollah. 2017.

Rammal, H., and M. A. S. Salameh. Hezbollah: Between Politics and Violence. 2017.

Rola, el-Husseini. "Resistance, Jihad, and martyrdom in contemporary Lebanese Shi'a discourse." Middle East Journal, 2008, doi: 10.3751/62.3.12.

Safieddine, Hicham. The Shi'ites of Lebanon: The Making of a Sect. 2003.

Sadiki, Louai. The Hizbullah Experience: The Party of God and its Socio-Political Roles in Lebanon. 2011.

Seliktar, O., Rezaei, F. (2020). Hezbollah in Lebanon: Creating the Model Proxy. In: Iran, Revolution, and Proxy Wars. Middle East Today. Palgrave Macmillan, Cham. https://doi.org/10.1007/978-3-030-29418-2_2

Smith, Charles. Terrorism: A History. New York: Wiley, 2006.

Smith, Mary A. Hezbollah and the Politics of Remembrance. 2013.

Tal, David. Hezbollah's Military Strategy and Operations: The Threat to Israel. 2018.

Tilly, Charles. Social Movements, 1768-2004. Paradigm Publishers, 2004.

Trenchard, T. (2011). Hezbollah in Transition: Moving From Terrorism to Political Legitimacy. https://doi.org/10.21236/ada560136.

Vahdat, Fatemeh. The Islamic Republic of Iran: A Theological Analysis of Resistance. Routledge, 2021.

Wahab, H. (2022). Hezbollah: A Regional Armed Non-State Actor (1st ed.). Routledge. https://doi.org/10.4324/9781003268826.

Zahar, Marie-Joelle. The Politics of the Lebanese Civil War between Hezbollah and the Lebanese State. 2009.

Zisser, Eyal. Hezbollah and the Emergence of Political Party: In Search of a Political Popularity. 2014.

Zisser, Eyal. Hezbollah and Iran: A Strategic Partnership for the Future. 2012.

Zoubir, Yahia H. Iran and Its Regional Security Policies: A Comprehensive Security Model. Routledge, 2008.

www.ingramcontent.com/pod-product-compliance
Lightning Source LLC
Chambersburg PA
CBHW031151020426
42333CB00013B/609